BERNADETTE McCARVER SNYDER

SAiNTLY

Celebrations

& HOLY

Holidays

**Easy and Imaginative
Ideas to Create
Your Own Catholic
Family Traditions**

Liguori
ONE LIGUORI DRIVE
LIGUORI MO 63057-9999
314.464.2500

ISBN 0-7648-0101-5
Library of Congress Catalog Card Number: 97-71703

Copyright © 1997, Bernadette McCarver Snyder
Printed in the United States of America
97 98 99 00 01 5 4 3 2 1

Cover design and interior art by Christine Kraus

INTRODUCTION

Sandpaper next to the sandwiches? Toy drums with the drumsticks? Marbles by the marmalade? What's all that stuff doing on the table where you serve dinner? No, the kids didn't do it. You did! Why? To celebrate holidays and holy days, to create do-it-yourself traditions, to make memories, and to have family fun!

Step back a moment into the once-upon-a-time happenings in your life. Is there a day that is filed away in that memory box in your head? A day at Grandma's…a "mystery" trip your Dad planned… a family picnic that had more sunshine than ants…a walk in the woods…a candlelit family holiday dinner…a jewel of a day or a moment that you will never forget? If you have one of those memories, treasure it. But whether you do or don't,

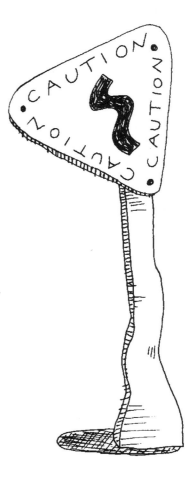

THERE'S STILL TIME TO MAKE SOME MEMORIES FOR YOURSELF AND YOUR FAMILY.

Even in today's hurried, harried world, no matter how busy you are, you can cook up family celebrations. And this book will show you how easy it can be. It offers a batch of pick-and-choose ways to put "red letter days" into every month of the year. All the ideas are practical and possible and have been family tested. And they're all fun!

Some of these ideas will be just right for your family. Maybe some will not. You decide which to try and which to pitch. And once you get started, you'll soon find lots of ways to add your own special touches to custom make family times special by adding just a pinch of imagination and a few sprinkles of time.

But please. Don't look through this book and then put it away and plan to start *some day*. Tomorrow is too late. Children grow up fast and days turn into years before you know it. This is the day the Lord has made for you to rejoice and be glad. So let the grass grow, let the laundry lay, let the phone ring. Today is the day to have family fun, to start to celebrate holidays and holy days, to delight in the moment, to cook up some memories.

A WORD OF CAUTION:

Celebrations do not always turn out the way you hoped. If your family at first doesn't appreciate your idea of family fun, keep at it anyway. Starting a family tradition is like planting a seed. It takes a little work and a little waiting before you get a bouquet. Sometimes you plan and plot and it seems no one appreciates your work or even enjoys it. But weeks later, or even *years* later, someone in the family will say, "You remember that wonderful day when we…" and you'll know it was worth the work and the wait.

DEDICATION

I dedicate this book to families of the past
who laid the foundation of traditions, rituals, and celebrations...
to families of the present who are adding
to the foundation with their own structures of faith and fun,
new doors that open both inward and outward, new skylights
that open upward, all happily built into everyday life...
and to families of the future who will continue to build,
adding their own new windows and walkways.

I dedicate this book to *my* family and to *yours*.

JANUARY

JANUARY

Saints' Days

This is the month to take a second look at the past and a first look at the future. Did you know the name *January* comes from an ancient Roman figure named Janus? Janus had two faces—one looking back, another looking forward. As you consider new beginnings for the year and for your family, look back at the meals and the times you shared last year. Could they have been more fun, more of a celebration? This year be an innovator, an originator. Become an ancestor. How do you do that? By starting your own family traditions. Read on…and enjoy.

Are there any "saints" in your family? Whenever you come to the feast day of someone's name-saint be sure to celebrate. Make a halo of silver foil for the "sainted" one. Read the story of the name-saint aloud. Have a special treat like round-like-a-halo pizza? (See FEBRUARY for more saint day celebration ideas. Hint: If you have any "angel hair" left over from Christmas, don't pack it away. Save it to use for "saintly" decorations.)

MAKE IT A TRADITION

Start your "new" traditions on the first day of the new year. Decide on something a little different to have for dinner, and serve that on *every* New Year's Day. Then in years to come, your children can look back and say, "On New Year's Day, we always ate...."

MAKE IT A CELEBRATION

Families do not live by food alone. Make the meal special, memorable, and "holy" too. Whatever you decide to serve, make the family gather around a celebration table: whether it's a dining room table, a kitchen table, or a card table. Cover it with a nice cloth, and in the center put a Bible or prayer book, flowers or a plant, and a group of candles: one for each person present. Instead of saying your usual blessing before meals, remind everyone that the first book of the Bible, the Book of Genesis, reads this way: "In the beginning, God created the heavens and the earth...." Explain that the new year is also a beginning, and ask each family member to light a candle and make a wish for this year. But instead of making a wish for himself or herself, make a wish for some *other* family member. Save these resolutions for dessert time when you will serve resolution cake!

Winter Picnic? Sure. Pack food in a picnic basket as usual. Serve it as you sit around a plastic tablecloth on the family room floor. Join hands and say a prayer of thanksgiving that there are no ants. Giggle and enjoy.

Will Rogers Said: "I figure there's no use being too particular. I don't care which side my bread is buttered on; I always eat both sides anyway." When you fix lunch, use cookie cutters to cut the bread into fancy shapes and the kids will think plain old bread-n-bologna or peanut butter-n-jelly sandwiches are more fun.

Bless You. When the January sniff-n-sneeze season hits, it's customary to say, "God bless you," to the sneezer. Did you know this custom began in 1665 when a terrible plague hit London? An early symptom of the disease was a sneeze. So "bless you" was a sincere prayer that the person would survive. Say "bless you" to someone today, even if no one sneezes.

Mmmm...mmmm.... Hot soup on a January night or hot chocolate on a January morning are as welcome as an old friend who drops in just when you need a shoulder to cry on. Share a cup of warmth and take time for a one-on-one chat with someone in your family this January.

Warm Up Winter. If you have a fireplace, sit around the fire. If not, sit around the kitchen table. Tell stories of how our great grandmothers spent winter evenings making quilts, roasting chestnuts, having taffy pulls. Talk about how Jesus' mother, Mary, and grandmother, Ann, may have spent winter evenings. Pop corn and munch while you read a children's Bible story.

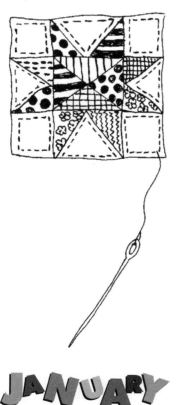

Serving suggestions: In the South it is a tradition to always include black-eyed peas in the New Year's Day meal. Here's a variation you might consider. Look for the dried bean section in the grocery store and buy a bag of "13 bean soup mix." Cooking directions are on the bag and it makes an easy, delicious, one-pot meal. You could add a pan of cornbread (made from a mix) and a green salad. Here's a bonus: The soup takes a couple of hours to simmer so the tantalizing aroma will remind the family that this is a special day, a "tradition" day.

But if your family doesn't like soup-y dinners, plan a simple but *fancy* meal. Stuff celery pieces with spreadable cheese for an appetizer. Grill a steak outside, even if it is snowing. Make a *different* salad by adding marinated artichokes or sliced pimiento or salted peanuts or whatever strikes your fancy. Or look through a recipe book and find one easy but unusual recipe that you will cook *only* that one day of the year. Whatever you serve, make it the same every year so it will become a family tradition. And then, you might like to end the New Year meal with resolution cake.

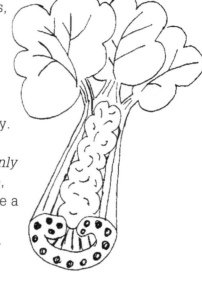

RESOLUTION CAKE

Ahead of time, look through family games to find game pieces: maybe a thimble, shoe, horse, or car. Or buy some small figures at a hobby shop or toy store. A few days before New Year's Day, put the pieces in a box and pass it around at suppertime. Ask each family member to choose the figure that could represent his or her resolution for the new year, but tell them to keep the resolution secret. You might give them suggestions to start them thinking. For example, *thimble:* I resolve to "sew" together a better relationship with my brother; *car:* I resolve to say one short prayer every time I "travel" in a car; *shoe:* I resolve to do chores or errands to save "steps" for Mom or Dad. Make your favorite cake or buy one at the grocery store. Decorate the top of the cake with the symbols chosen. Put the cake on a nice platter or tray and surround it with New Year decorations: confetti, streamers, party hats, noise makers. At dessert time, cut the cake and give each person the piece with the symbol he or she has chosen. Each person can either announce the resolution or remember it silently. For the rest of the year, whenever you serve cake ask, "Do you remember our resolution cake? Are you keeping your resolutions?" This could lead to groans or giggles but it will reinforce the idea of tradition.

ONCE UPON A TIME...

Children love for you to take time to read stories with them. Make it a custom, once a week if possible, to have "family" story time. Read from a favorite book, and then tell one of your own once-upon-a-time stories about when you were a child or a teenager. Include stories about church happenings too: baptisms, weddings, Easter, Christmas....

DATE DAYS

Choose a gray, drab day to sit down and note on your *new* calendar all the birthdays and anniversaries of family and friends for the year. Try to track down baptism dates and mark those too. Then you can celebrate both.

BAPTISM DAY CELEBRATIONS

To celebrate the *water* of baptism, buy an inexpensive but fancy-looking set of water glasses and use them *only* on baptism days. Or celebrate further by having a family swimming party—at an outdoor pool in summer, at an indoor pool when the weather is cold. Or celebrate by driving your car through a car wash and then going to a drive-in restaurant for burgers. Who says celebrating a serious religious anniversary has to be *serious*? Just remember to stress *why* you are celebrating water, and make it a happy time to remember. On baptism days, serve a fun dessert like the following winter surprise.

ESKIMO 1-2-3 SURPRISE!

#1. In your grocer's frozen dessert section look for those summertime goodies that are squares or rectangles of vanilla ice cream covered with crisp chocolate. Buy one for each person to be "dessert-ed." #2. If you get the kind that come on a stick, remove the stick. Chunk up each ice cream bar into an individual dessert dish. #3. Drizzle over each some store-bought caramel sauce or green mint jelly, and top with a maraschino cherry. It looks fancy and tastes "delish" and the lucky "dessert-ers" will wonder how you fixed it so fast.

<u>Fortune Cupcakes?</u> Instead of fortune cookies, buy or make some cupcakes, then cut a little slit in the side of each one. On small slips of paper, write questions about some virtue: Do you always keep your promises? Do you always tell the truth? Do you say a prayer *every* day? Or ask "think" questions: Who is your best friend and why? What is your favorite prayer and why? Why do you like or not like to go to church on Sunday? Fold each slip of paper and slide it into a cupcake. Since the family may "challenge" each answer, keep it light; keep it fun. You may learn some new things about each other.

Change-ing Times. In fourteenth-century Europe, pin makers only sold pins on January 1 and 2. Since few women had money of their own in those days, husbands would give their wives "pin" money. Resolve this year to put aside a bit of pin money each week and by next Christmas you'll have enough to buy a surprise present for someone outside your family circle who seldom receives gifts.

Veg-out. Spend a family evening looking through seed catalogues or a gardening book, and do some "armchair" planting. Discuss why you think God made the kinds of vegetables he did and what kinds of vegetables you might have preferred. Chomp on some celery and carrot sticks while you talk. And for the non-veggie members, have a bag of pretzels.

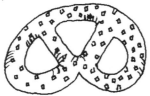

Poetry. On January 4, 1774, Phyllis Wheatley, a former slave, became the first established American black author by publishing *Poems*. Read (or write) some poems today.

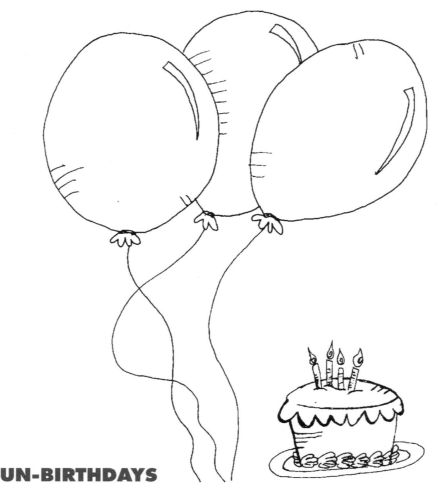

UN-BIRTHDAYS

Sometimes you need to celebrate when there's no special date on the calendar. That's when you can have an *un*-birthday party. Since it's nobody's special day, you can honor everybody. Buy enough helium balloons for each party person. Put each balloon into a brown grocery bag, and staple or tape the bag closed. Use a magic marker to label each bag with one person's name. Have a simple dinner and an un-birthday cake, and then present your gifts. As each person opens a bag, a balloon will float out and soon the room will be full of people chasing balloons. If you feel generous you could tie a small gag gift on each balloon string. After the chase, tie all the balloons into a "bouquet," and take them the next day to a children's hospital to be given to some small patient.

While you are enjoying the un-birthday cake, talk about the highflying balloons, and mention that we are all filled with the Holy Spirit just as the balloons are filled with helium. Suggest that we too could soar and fly if we would listen to the Spirit and always be aware that we are God-filled.

THE KINGS ARE COMING!

Don't take the Christmas tree down until it's time to celebrate Twelfth Night, Epiphany, the coming of the Wise Men on January 6. For young children, have a wise-and-wonderful party. Help the children make invitations with crayon drawings of crowns. Distribute these to friends. Dress three children as the Wise Men with "royal" bathrobes, paper crowns, Mommy's jewelry. They can greet guests as they arrive and then all gather around the tree or crib to read or act out the story of the Magi. It will be more fun if you use props to illustrate the story: a big silver star of aluminum foil, a treasure chest full of "gold" coins, incense to burn for the frankincense, and for the myrrh, a container of nice-smelling cream sachet or lotion into which all can dip their fingers. After the story, let the three kings lead guests to the refreshment table, possibly taking the long-way-round through bedrooms and hallways to make it a journey. Serve cold punch or hot spiced tea and a cake decorated with a "crown" made of brightly-colored gumdrops. You could play simple games and award prizes wrapped in gold or silver foil and bright ribbons. And you could give each child a paper crown to wear home: just scallop the edges of a lunch bag and decorate with glued-on sequins.

Camel Food. There is an old Spanish custom for children to celebrate the eve of January 6 by leaving a pile of straw outside for the Wise Men's camels. The next morning, the straw would be gone, replaced by a pile of small goodies—a return gift from the Magi.

Teachers and Students. On January 6, 1907, Maria Montessori, Italy's first woman physician, opened the first Montessori school for young children. At dinnertime say a special prayer for all teachers and all school children.

Martin Luther King, Jr. January 16 is the birthday of Dr. Martin Luther King, Jr., the civil rights leader who made the famous "I have a dream..." speech. Ask the family, "What is *your* dream and why?"

For older children, have a royal Magi party. Make it a very elegant dinner party with a royal purple (or white) tablecloth, candles, flowers, or whatever you can gather to make it look special. In contrast to the fancy decorations, keep it a "family" affair by serving meatloaf. But make the meatloaf in the shape of a crown, and trim it with golden triangles of cheese and pimiento "jewels."

YOU NEED A PARTY PANTRY OR A TRADITION TRUNK

Family celebrations can sometimes be pulled together with whatever's on hand plus a bit of creativity. But some festivities require a few special ingredients. Since you are starting family traditions which you will do every year, you need to save some things from year to year. If you don't already have one, find a spot in the basement or a storage room where you can keep a few labeled boxes for your supplies. You might also want to save a pantry shelf where you can keep simple staples for "instant" celebrations: cake mix, canned icing, food coloring.

FEBRUARY

FEBRUARY

Saints' Days

3 **Blaise**
5 **Agatha**
6 **Paul Miki and Companions**
10 **Scholastica**
14 **Cyril and Methodius**
21 **Peter Damian**
23 **Polycarp of Smyrna**

Welcome to a short month with lots of chances to celebrate. There's the feast of the Presentation, Groundhog Day, Valentine's Day, Washington's and Lincoln's birthdays. And in many years, this month also includes Ash Wednesday, the beginning of Lent—a time to "celebrate" prayer and look forward to spring and Easter.

I never saw a moor,
I never saw the sea;
Yet know I how the heather looks
And what a wave must be.

Emily Dickinson

In this wintry month of February, it may be hard to envision springtime, but God has promised us new life. Every year, the bare tree branches bud forth with new leaves and the jonquils bloom. God never fails to keep any promises made.

HOLY LIGHTS

February 2 is the feast of the Presentation. When Jesus was born, it was the custom for newborn babies and new mothers to go to the Temple to be "presented" to God and to receive special blessings. This is also the day when candles are blessed to be used during the coming year so it is sometimes called Candlemas Day. You will need some unblessed candles for the next family idea. Read on....

IT'S DARK IN HERE!

Before February 2, look on your bookshelf or go to the library to find an animal book that includes information about the groundhog. Serve "Groundhog" sausage and scrambled eggs for supper. After supper, gather in a circle on the floor and read about the groundhog. Then turn off all the lights. Pretend to be groundhogs, asleep in a little dark hole. Next pretend to be waking up. Stretch and yawn. Act like it's just the first rays of dawn. Light some candles and see if you can "see" your shadow. Then look through the animal book, and read about other animals too. Talk about the many, many animals God made and how they are all so different (just like he made so many people and how they are each so different). For a snack, pass out animal crackers and ask each child which is his or her favorite animal and why?

WELL, BLESS MY THROAT!

According to legend, a bishop named Blaise once saved the life of a little boy who was choking on a fish bone. On the feast of Saint Blaise, February 3, or on the Sunday nearest, most Catholic churches have a religious ceremony known as the Blessing of Throats. The priest crosses two unlit candles, puts them under your throat, and says a prayer asking God to keep you healthy. Have a candlelit dinner, and say a prayer asking God to bless all the family throats this year.

SEEING DOUBLE

Twins are twice as nice. On February 10 we celebrate the feast of Saint Scholastica who was the twin sister of Saint Benedict. He founded the Benedictine Order of Monks and she founded the Benedictine Order of Nuns. To honor these twin saints, serve double-decker sandwiches for dinner with double-dip ice-cream cones for dessert. If you know any twins invite them over to share in the celebration.

Our Lady of Lourdes. February 11 is the feast day of Our Lady of Lourdes. Observe this feast by having a movie night. Rent the video of the old Hollywood movie *The Song of Bernadette* which tells the story of this saint and the miracles of Lourdes. Don't forget to serve popcorn. Since Saint Bernadette was French, maybe you could also serve something French for dinner: French bread or croissants, French pastry, or French-fried potatoes.

Abraham Lincoln said: "Die when I may, I want it said by those who knew me best that I always plucked a thistle and planted a flower where I thought a flower would grow." Sometimes we spend more time trying to pluck thistles or weeds from our garden of life than we do in planting flowers.

A Positive Lent. Instead of "giving up" something for Lent this year, turn *shall not* into *shall*. Think of something good you should do but that you hate doing. Then do it every day during Lent. Maybe the family will follow your example.

Family Patches. Quilts have become popular again and there are wonderful names for the patterns: the *wedding ring*, the *9-patch*, the *wild-goose chase*. In the past, when ladies regularly attended quilting bees, they could all use the same kinds of pieces but each finished quilt would look totally different. It's the same with a family. The Lord sends us "pieces" but we cut 'em and put 'em together in different ways. And the cutting and the patching make the difference. That's why each family is unique.

Did You Know? It takes 3,750 crocus flowers to make one ounce of saffron? Didn't God have a wild way of putting spice into our world?

A closed mouth gathers no foot.

TIME FOR A HEART-Y PARTY

February 14 is an easy day to celebrate. Buy or bake heart cookies or a heart cake. If you don't have a heart-shaped cake pan you can make a heart cake easily by baking a cake-mix cake in one square pan and one round pan. Let the cakes cool, then remove them from the pans. Place the square cake so that it looks like a diamond; cut the round cake in half, and place each half at the upper two edges of the diamond. Voila! A heart shape. Ice with white frosting and top with Valentine heart candies. If you use the candies that have messages on them, maybe everyone will want to read the cake before they eat it.

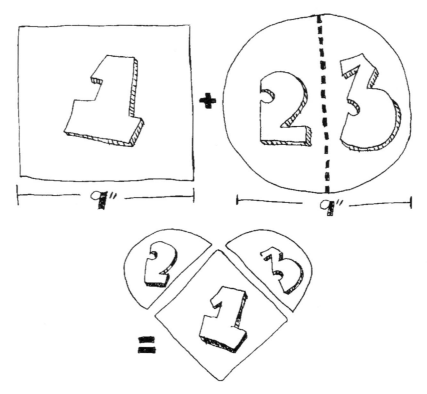

Or instead of a heart dessert you could make a Valentine meatloaf. Just pour the meat mixture into a shallow pan and shape it like a heart. Then bake as usual. The kids will probably make fun of it, but it will taste as good as usual and give everyone a good laugh.

Also this day will give you an opportunity to talk about how some people are lonely and don't have anyone to love them or send them a Valentine. Discuss people you know who might be in greatest need of some "Tender Loving Care" (TLC) and how you could make it a family project to be "Valentines" for a day, a week, or a month. You could invite the person to dinner, send cards, notes or gift coupons, secretly leave little gifts on the doorstep, and so on. This could become a yearly tradition—planning ahead each year *who* you will choose as the "Valentine Person" to receive some TLC.

WHOSE FEAST IS THIS ANYWAY?

Although we think of February 14 as Saint Valentine's Day, according to the liturgical calendar, it is really the feast of two brothers, Saints Cyril and Methodius. Cyril was a monk, missionary, and teacher who invented a Yugoslavian alphabet. Methodius helped his brother translate the gospels using this new alphabet. You probably won't be able to find any "Happy Saints Cyril and Methodius" cards but you can serve some alphabet soup for lunch along with the Valentines.

LINCOLN LETTERS

To celebrate Lincoln's birthday, get a batch of Lincoln-head pennies. Help the children make greeting cards using squares of construction paper or index cards. Glue a penny on the card and use it as the beginning of a design. The penny can be the center of a flower or the head of a stick figure. Using crayons or ballpoint pens, the kids will probably come up with lots of imaginative designs. Send these cards to that special "Valentine Person" you chose earlier or to grandparents, out-of-town relatives, or anyone.

BY GEORGE!

Of course, George Washington's birthday is the time to serve cherry pie in honor of George chopping down the cherry tree. But you could also serve a "By George" brownie. Top a chocolate brownie with canned cherry pie filling and a dollop of whipped topping. While enjoying this easy two-minutes-to-make dessert, talk about how things have changed since George Washington's day. End the meal by saying a prayer for all politicians and world leaders.

A Timely Tip. The word "tip" (meaning something extra you give to someone who has given you good service) was originally an acronym meaning "To Insure Promptness." How many in your family need a tip to insure promptness?

From Cook to Book. Abigail Fillmore, wife of President Millard Fillmore, arranged for the purchase of the first cooking stove in the White House. She also set up the first White House Library. Woman does not live by stove alone!

A Kiss for My Book! In some homes in India, books are so treasured it is a custom that if you drop a book (especially a "holy" book), you not only pick it up quickly but also kiss it as an apology for the disrespect of dropping it. Read to the family a chapter from a holy book today.

<u>Chip Chop.</u> A fast way to make a plain cake fancy for a birthday or any occasion honoring a special person is to "write" the person's name on the cake using chocolate chips or red-hot cinnamon candies.

<u>Hot Diggity Dog?</u> If you have some extra hot dog buns, surprise the kids with a no-dog hot dog. Peel a banana and put it in the bun. Then instead of adding mustard and relish, let the kids add their own peanut butter, honey, jelly, or even mayonnaise or mustard if they insist.

<u>Exuberance.</u> William Blake said, "Exuberance is beauty." Even if you're in the midst of a February snow storm, try to live today with exuberance. Maybe it will make you look or feel more beautiful.

TIME IS GOLDEN

Did you ever hear of having a golden year birthday celebration? A golden year is the year when you are the same age as the date you were born. If you were born on the 10th of the month, you celebrate your golden year birthday when you are 10 years old. If you were born on the 24th of the month, you have to wait until you are 24. And if you are already older than 31, it's too late to celebrate. A golden year birthday means a year of good luck, and it certainly starts out that way since people are supposed to bring presents that are *golden*. Plan to have golden year birthday celebrations in the future if you can match up anyone with the proper year. Remind the family, and yourself, that every year God gives us is golden.

SUBSTITUTE GOLDEN

Even if there are no golden year birthdays on your calendar this year, you can make any Sunday golden by serving golden scallop shells. Simply take one large orange for each two people to be served. Cut *just the skin* of the orange around the center with a knife point as though you were going to cut it in half. Push a spoon handle between the meaty pulp of the orange and the skin. Work all the way around until you can remove the inside of the orange and save the skin of both halves. (If you have small oranges you will need to cut nearer to the top and use one whole orange shell for each person.) Use scissors to scallop the edges of the shells to make little cups. Fill each cup with ice cream or orange sherbet and serve for dessert.

Or make mashed sweet potatoes (flavored with brown sugar, butter, and just a pinch of nutmeg), and pile the potatoes into the orange shells and warm them in the oven. This may sound hard but it only takes a few minutes and the kids will love them. These could easily become a tradition for Sunday meals.

And here's a bonus: Take the orange "insides" and mix with canned pineapple and chopped maraschino cherries and/or coconut. Chill and you'll have tomorrow night's dessert all ready.

SPEAKING OF SUNDAY

Try to always make Sunday special: a day to rejoice in the Lord's day. If all the family can't be together for a noon or evening meal, plan a special breakfast or brunch. The food can be simple but it can seem fancy if you use a tablecloth and some kind of centerpiece.

The centerpiece can be as simple as a few fresh flowers or a green plant or you can be creative. Choose something that will tie in with the time of year (hearts for February) or a saint's feast day (a statue or a holy picture) or some family event (family photos or mementos). When all else fails you can simply use a group of leftover candles of whatever size to "brighten" up the meal.

It's a good idea to buy a small (for example, 8- by 10-inch) rectangular or round mirror and use it as the base for your centerpiece. This reflects well, makes whatever you put on it look special, and sets it aside from the food. And you can get the children involved. Occasionally let them choose what you should feature as the Sunday centerpiece. The small ones might ask you to use a favorite teddy bear or doll, toy or lunchbox. So why not? It's all in the family.

SAINTLY CELEBRATIONS

If you have celebrated a saint's name by giving it to a family member, it is only proper that you should celebrate that saint's feast. In this book, you'll find a list of saint days for each month so you can plan ahead. The day before, gather the family to make a simple banner. Just cut a square or rectangle of felt or heavy fabric, and use a marker to write on it, "Happy Saint Polycarp Day" or the name of whatever saint you are celebrating. If you know anything about the saint you could add that too: a rose for Theresa, a crown for David, a lion for Daniel. Hang this in a prominent place, ready to observe the feast.

Let the name-day person choose what you will have for dinner. For a centerpiece, use a glob of angel hair or cotton, and put a statue of the saint in the middle of it. If you don't have a statue use a saint picture, a cross, a rosary, or cut out some symbol to represent the saint. After dinner, read or tell the story of the saint's life. If it is a well-known story, let one of the children tell it.

A Wintertime "Cooler." Put fresh fruit (strawberries, sliced banana) or canned fruit into tall glasses. Fill each glass with lemonade (made from a mix or a frozen concentrate), and top with a scoop of ice cream or sherbet. As you enjoy the "cool," ask the family to pretend you are all together on a summer "dream vacation." Then ask each one, "In your dream, where are we?" It will be fun to find out if you are each at a different place.

Notes

_____

_____

_____

_____

_____

_____

_____

_____

_____

_____

_____

_____

_____

_____

_____

_____

MARDI GRAS TIME!

Carnivals or Mardi Gras parties are often held on the days before Ash Wednesday—which sometimes comes in February, sometimes in March. People dress up in fancy costumes and have parades and eat fancy foods because during Lent they plan to do more praying than partying. The words _Mardi Gras_ actually mean "fat Tuesday." So why don't you start the tradition of having a fat Tuesday party? Let the children dress in costumes but instead of serving fancy foods, serve frozen waffles or pancakes with lots of butter and syrup or canned fruit toppings and whipped cream. Talk to the children about why we observe Lent each year. Explain that we make sacrifices to prepare for Holy Week when Jesus made the greatest sacrifice of all—giving up his life for us.

AN ASH WEDNESDAY ALLELUIA

Talk again about Lent and how it will end with the alleluia time of Easter. Get out the crayons, glue, sequins, poster board, or felt, and make a fancy alleluia poster. Choose one family member to _hide the alleluia._ Be sure no one sees where it is hidden. Then, on Easter morning, make a big deal out of _finding the alleluia._ Bring out the poster and use it as an Easter decoration.

BE A LAMB

If there are small children in the family, trace the outline of a lamb on a piece of poster board, and then let the children add the lamb's "wool" by gluing on a piece of popcorn or a cotton ball each day of Lent. Use the finished lamb as part of your Easter decorations.

MARCH

MARCH

Saints' Days

4 **Casimir**
7 **Perpetua and Felicity**
8 **John of God**
9 **Frances of Rome**
15 **Clement Hofbauer**
17 **Patrick**
18 **Cyril of Jerusalem**
19 **Joseph**
23 **Turibius of Mongrovejo**

Sure and begorrah! Here comes Saint Patrick's month plus Saint Joseph's feast day and Lenten days and maybe even Easter which sometimes comes in March, sometimes in April.

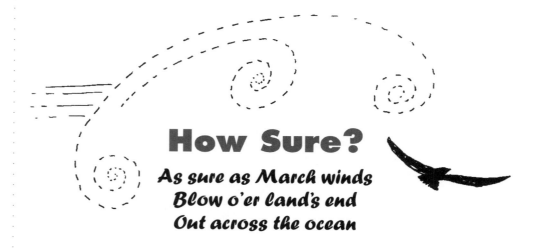

How Sure?

As sure as March winds
Blow o'er land's end
Out across the ocean

Can down a sailor rough, raw, and blue
But lift a gull with tender hue,
As soothing as a lotion.

G. B. Riler

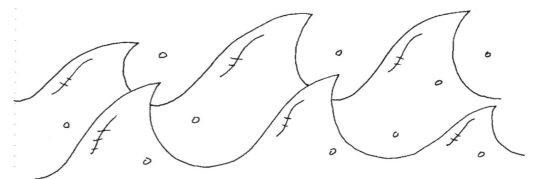

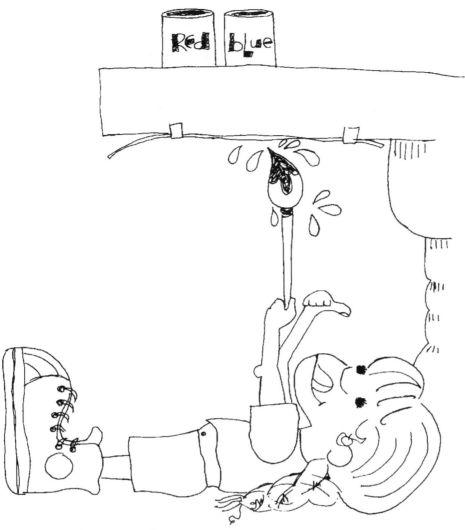

March is a time to *enjoy* crowds.

"Wisdom begins in wonder." Socrates

New Life. March is the month when tiny green sprouts begin to peep forth from the winter earth and tiny buds appear on the trees. This is the time to point out to the children the wonder of God's creation and how God keeps the promise of new life and sends springtime every year. Or maybe they'll point it out to you!

"We do not see things as *they* are. We see things as *we* are." The Talmud

LOOKING UP!

March 6 is the birthday of Michelangelo, the famous artist who painted the fabulous scenes on the ceiling of the Sistine Chapel in Rome. Here's an idea for the nearest Saturday to this date or for an after-school activity. If possible, find a book with some pictures of Michelangelo's paintings to show the children. If not, just tell them about the beautiful chapel ceiling and how the artist had to paint it by laying on his back on scaffolding. Then tape some plain white paper on the *under*side of an old card table or the kitchen table. Give the kids some crayons, and tell them to pretend by lying down under the table and reaching up to draw some religious pictures of God or Jesus or the apostles. While they are drawing, fix some sandwiches for lunch (if it's Saturday) or some kind of snack. When they finish drawing, tell them it's time to have a "tent" picnic. Let them sit under the table to eat and admire their artwork. Sit on the floor with them, and talk about how many famous artists drew religious pictures. If you have a book of religious art, look through it and let each child choose his or her favorite painting.

Why are eggs so happy? Because they keep their sunny side up.

How many eggs can a hen lay? A hard-boiled hen can lay up to 250 eggs a year...and that's no yolk.

WEARIN' OF THE GREEN

No one has to tell you how to celebrate March 17—wear green clothes, serve corned beef and cabbage or some kind of *green* food (the kids might not be excited if you choose broccoli or brussels sprouts but they might like green gelatin or green bagels with cream cheese), take the kids to a Saint Patrick's Day parade, and buy a pot of green shamrocks for a centerpiece.

Or you could let the kids make a shamrock centerpiece. (Do this a few days *before* Saint Patrick's Day.) Just get a small shamrock pattern and cut out quite a few using green construction paper. On one shamrock, lay a broom straw or a kabob spear, and hold it in place with a bit of tape. Put a dab of glue on the tape, and glue another shamrock on the back of the first one. You will have two shamrocks glued together with a long stem between them. Let the kids make as many as they like until your time, material, and patience runs out. Set the shamrocks aside to dry, and then put them into a vase or a green container, and use as a decorative centerpiece for your Irish dinner.

THREE-IN-ONE

Don't forget to tell the children *why* we think of the shamrock as "Irish." Tell them about the legend that Saint Patrick used the shamrock to teach the Irish people about the Holy Trinity by showing that the shamrock is a three-in-one leaf just as the Holy Trinity is three-in-one: three persons—Father, Son, and Holy Spirit—in one God.

IRISH PROVERB

Cabbage, like a good wife, is often taken for granted.
If the kids don't like cabbage cut in wedges and boiled with new potatoes, try giving them creamed cabbage. Just buy a package of cole slaw mix in the produce department, but don't make slaw. Instead, put the cabbage mix into a bowl with a bit of water, and cook it in the microwave until it is just soft, but not mushy. Drain any water off. Buy or make a cream sauce (you can find the easy recipe in most cookbooks), and stir it into the cabbage mixture.

AN IRISH LEPRECHAUN TRICK

Try this for breakfast or dinner on Saint Patrick's Day. Have the table all set with some nice clear water glasses. Don't let anyone see you put a tiny dab of green food coloring in the bottom of each glass. Have a cold pitcher of water or apple juice ready to pour, and as soon as everyone sits down announce that sometimes a very wonderful thing happens on Saint Patrick's Day. Quickly fill each glass and as you pour, the liquid will "magically" change from clear to green! Explain that this only happens on Saint Patrick's Day and only once per person—no seconds. Don't ever tell your secret and you might get by with it for several years.

Surprise Eggs. Take some sharp skinny object like a hat pin or a skewer, and make a small hole in one end of an uncooked egg. Then make a slightly larger hole in the other end, being sure to pierce the egg yolk inside. Hold the egg over a bowl, and carefully blow into the small hole. The egg should all come out into the bowl leaving the shell intact. Rinse the shell with warm water, and put it in an egg carton, large hole down, to dry. "Empty" six eggs in this way. Use the eggs for cooking or to scramble. When the six egg shells are dry, turn them up so the large hole will be at the top. Mix two envelopes of *unflavored* gelatin with one 3-ounce package of fruit-flavored gelatin. Add 1 1/2 cups boiling water, and stir until all is dissolved. Let cool for 10 minutes. Pour the gelatin into a pitcher with a spout, and carefully fill each egg. Refrigerate until set. Won't everyone be surprised when they break the shell and, instead of a hard-boiled egg, they find a jiggly gelatin egg! (Note: This really is *not* hard to make.)

<u>Get Cracking!</u> To get the kernel of a nut, you first have to crack the shell. When a child seems troubled, be alert; be available. Take time to chat, to listen, to watch. Try to understand before you criticize. Try to solve little problems before they turn into big ones.

<u>Food Faces Are Fun!</u> Kids love it when you put a happy face on lunch. Make a face on an open-face bologna sandwich by using olive slices for eyes, a triangle of cheese for a nose, and a strip of pickle or pimiento (out of the olive) for the mouth. Turn a canned peach half cut-side down, and make a face with raisin eyes, a cherry nose, an apple slice or a row of raisins for a mouth. Smile!

LENT AND REPENT?

Children will not understand the significance of Lent unless you explain it to them. You can talk about this being a special time of prayer or for doing something special to show Jesus you want to sacrifice and share in his suffering and thank him for *his* sacrifice for you. A longtime Lenten practice has been to "give up" eating candy or desserts or to "give up" some bad habit. Some other Lenten suggestions you might make to the children: do chores without having to be reminded over and over; be more reverent about bedtime prayers; be more careful about school work; be more thoughtful and considerate of brothers and sisters *and* parents.

SACRIFICE SUPPERS

Suggest to the family that you have a week of Lenten sacrifice suppers. If they agree, shop carefully and buy only simple, inexpensive food so you can spend only half of your usual weekly grocery budget. The simple meals could include: soup (canned or homemade) with bread and green salad; hamburger casserole with slaw or gelatin salad; or tuna casserole with canned fruit salad. And do without cookies, chips, and other snack foods for the week. Write out a check for the money you saved, and let one of the children drop it in the collection basket on Sunday or mail it to a charity or buy a basket of food and give it to a poor family. The kids may complain about the simple dinners but later they will probably brag about how they "sacrificed." They may even want to do this as a regular family project when it's not Lent.

LENTEN CENTERPIECE

Here's an idea for a Lenten centerpiece for the sacrifice suppers or any meal: use a big piece of sandpaper, some rocks from the garden or a few nails, and a purple candle or a pot of cactus. Eyes will roll but it will be a reminder that Lent is supposed to be a time to do hard things instead of easy things.

GIVE US THIS DAY OUR DAILY BREAD

March 19 is the feast of Saint Joseph, the "breadwinner" for the Holy Family. Because of this, many Catholic churches have a special celebration this day and decorate the altar with fancy, twisty loaves of bread. After Mass, they give out rolls or small loaves of bread to those present. So this would be a good day to "start loafing."

START LOAFING

The word "lady" means "loaf giver." So be a lady. Buy some frozen bread dough and surprise your family with the fresh-baked aroma of homemade bread for dinner. If you want to be a super lady, bake an extra loaf, wrap it in plastic wrap and a ribbon, and give it to a friend. Or if you don't have time to bake, buy a very special, fancy, twisty loaf of bread from a good bakery, and put it in the center of the table as your centerpiece. Talk about today being Saint Joseph's Day. Cut the bread and share it. Talk about how the family members could share some "bread" (money) with the poor by chipping in a bit from their allowance. The Saint Joseph bread tradition is an easy and delicious one to establish.

"Whatever you have, spend less." Samuel Johnson

A Sticky Subject. Buy some flat wooden sticks at a craft store. When you are making cookies, insert a stick in a few and have lollipop cookies. Pour fruit yogurt into small paper cups, add a stick in each, freeze, and you have yogurt on a stick. Show the kids how to use these sticks to make "log" cabins. Or find a holy picture and glue a stick on all four sides to make a frame.

Choo Choo. A family is like a train. All the "cars" have to pull together and go in the same direction or you'll never get anywhere.

Rock Concert. Take the children to a park, and look for some "pretty" and smooth rocks. At home, use magic markers to decorate the rocks with faces, flowers, or sayings. You can write on the front of one rock "Turn me over" and on the other side write "Thanks, that feels good." The kids can use these to give as Easter gifts or birthday gifts or any-day gifts. Kids like to give gifts almost as much as they like to get them. Or maybe more.

Chinese Proverb: "Nothing is so full of victory as patience." It isn't easy to be patient with a houseful of family. But the only way to *teach* patience is to *be* patient, or at least to *act* patient.

THIS IS YOUR ANGEL SPEAKING

On March 25 we celebrate the feast of the Annunciation or "announcement" day—the day an angel appeared to Mary and told her she had been chosen to be the mother of Jesus. Tell the children this story, and talk about how surprised Mary must have been when the angel suddenly appeared and said, "Hail Mary" the way we would say, "Hello Mary" to a friend. Say the Hail Mary prayer together, then talk about angels. If you haven't talked about this before, explain how many people believe that each person has his or her own special guardian angel, sent by God. If the children don't know the guardian angel prayer, this would be a good day to start teaching it. Encourage them to make it a practice to say this prayer every morning when they first wake up.

Angel of God,
my guardian dear,
to whom [God's] love
commits me here,
ever this day (night),
be at my side,
to light and guard,
to rule and guide.

PRAYER PRETZELS?

Speaking of prayers, Lent is the perfect time to tell the children the story of the pretzel. In early Christian days, people kept a very strict fast all during Lent: no milk, butter, cheese, eggs, cream, or meat. And their "Lenten bread" was made with only flour, water, and salt. As a reminder that Lent was a time of prayer, the bread makers would shape the bread in the form of arms crossed in prayer. At that time, people crossed their arms over the chest while praying—just the way today's pretzels are shaped.

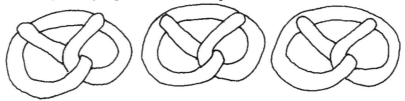

The monks usually taught prayers to the children so they made very small bits of bread into the "praying arms" shape and gave these "pretzels" as rewards to the children when they learned their prayers. Why don't you put a pretzel at each dinner plate all during Lent as a daily reminder that Lent is a time of prayer. This is another easy way to start a yearly tradition.

PLAN AHEAD

This takes a little preparation but some families have started the tradition of having a Seder supper or Passover meal on Holy Thursday. You might like to invite friends to share in this remembrance of the kind of meal that was served in Jesus' time. At each person's place, put a small bowl of salted water, a plate with a matzo cracker, a piece of parsley, and a small bowl that contains a mixture of chopped apples and raisins sprinkled with cinnamon. At the beginning of the meal, the mother or father lights some candles and says a little prayer. The leader pours a glass of wine or grape juice for each person. All raise their glasses and take a sip. Then the bitter herb (the parsley) is dipped into the salt water and eaten in memory of the tears and bitter suffering of the Hebrew slaves. The apple, raisin, and cinnamon mixture is eaten as a reminder of the mortar used by the slaves to build the Pharaoh's pyramids. Then the matzo is eaten to represent the unleavened bread the Israelites took with them when they fled into the desert. Now the glasses are raised again for another sip. Then the story of the deliverance from Egypt is told or read from the Book of Exodus, chapter 12. The traditional main course is lamb. You could serve lamb stew or you could just fix a simple casserole and salad. The kids will enjoy the ritual and solemnity of this tradition and can relax and have fun during the main course. (Note: This is a very simplified version of the Seder and easy to manage. But if you would like to hold a truly traditional meal, you could find complete instructions and recipes at the public library.)

<u>Butter up.</u> Did you know margarine was once *against the law*? When it was first introduced in America, dairy farmers did not like the competition. In many states, it was against the law to manufacture, sell, or color margarine yellow (so it would look like butter). Instead, it was sometimes colored PINK! Treat yourself to a margarine (or butter) and jelly sandwich. Put your feet up and enjoy. And say a prayer of thanks for American supermarkets and the wonderful variety of foods we have today.

HOT CROSS BUNS

Here's one of the oldest and most popular Lenten traditions: hot cross buns for breakfast on Good Friday or Holy Saturday. You can make your own or you can find them in many grocery stores and bakeries all during Lent. Make a ceremony of having everyone solemnly, not hurriedly, make the Sign of the Cross before they dig into the cross-shaped icing on the buns. If you have any holy water in the house, you might even have each person dip their fingers into it before making the Sign of the Cross.

HAVE AN MNEMONIC NIGHT

To show children how each is special, spend a night making up a positive "mnemonic device" of sorts for the initials of each child. For example, Ann Susan Harris would have the initials ASH: Always Sunshine Happy. Kevin Matthew Adams would have the initials KMA: Knows Math Answers. Matthew Daniel Smith would have the initials MDS: Million Dollar Smiles. The kids will enjoy making them up for each other, so encourage them to create ones that will "build up" instead of "put down" self-esteem. This can be a lot of fun.

YOU'LL FIND MORE HOLY WEEK AND EASTER IDEAS IN APRIL!

APRIL

APRIL

Saints' Days

pril showers bring May flowers… and April Fool's Day and sometimes Holy Week and Easter and birds and bunnies and "beyutiful" days.

Recipe for a happy family: Mix equal amounts of faith, love, understanding, and forgiveness. Sprinkle liberally with laughter. Serve daily in generous helpings.

APRIL FOOL

The first day of April is a time when people play silly jokes on each other. Do you know why? No one actually knows the real story. But here is one version.

Before the year 1564, French people celebrated New Year's Day on April l. But in 1564, the king of France adopted the "new" calendar which we use today and decreed that his people should celebrate January l as the beginning of the new year. Many people did *not* want to change so they did not observe January l as New Year's Day and they were called "April Fools."

Also, at that time, it was the custom to exchange New Year's gifts on April l so after the calendar changed, they still gave gifts on that day but they started giving silly gifts. Or they would wrap the gift to look like something different than what it was: a huge box that held a tiny gift or a long skinny box that held a short square gift. And that was the start of the April Fool joke. It's fun to play April Fool jokes as long as they are not mean jokes or jokes that might hurt someone.

On this day, you might also mention to the children that when Jesus was on earth, some people thought he was a fool. He taught people to *love your neighbor as yourself* and if someone hurts you, *turn the other cheek*. He didn't try to make a lot of money so he could live in a fancy house. He had friends who were not the most popular people in town. He even touched lepers at a time when no one would get near them. Finally, instead of saving himself, he died on the cross to save others. Ask the children, "Do you think Jesus was a fool?"

AN APRIL FOOL FAMILY GAME

On this night, play a familiar family game: cards or any board game, but have April Fool rules. At the end of each "hand" or "round," add a new rule. #1. Everyone flip a coin and if you get heads, double your score; if you get tails, cut your score in half. #2. Add l point for each slice of bread you ate today. #3. If you got up before 7 a.m., add 10 points to your score; if you got up after 7 a.m., deduct 10 points; if you said a prayer when you got up, add 100 points. #4. If you did a good deed for anyone today, add 200 points. Make up whatever kind of rules you think would be fun for your family. But be sure that a few rules include prayers or good deeds.

"A man who from his childhood can remember good things is saved for his entire life." Dostoyevsky

Keep your temper. Nobody else wants it.

Why are roosters "well-groomed" birds?

Because they always have their "combs" with them.

On old legend says that the egg is a symbol of the universe. The shell represents the sky; the shell "lining" (or membrane), the air; the white, the oceans and the waters; and the yolk, earth.

If we are Christians, why have we de-Christianized our lives? We should not only "put Christ back into Christmas," but also into every family celebration, every holiday, and everyday life.

That's what the English call it when they fill up on junk food or fun food. When the kids start stuffing down all that Easter candy, tell them they've become gobstoppers!

A Tree on the Table? In recent years, it has become popular to have an Easter tree as the centerpiece on your table. You can buy these or you can find a nice dry branch and spray paint it white or yellow or whatever bright color you like. Anchor it in a bowl or basket with clay, a styrofoam block, or something heavy enough to keep it from tipping over. Then let the children help you choose little decorations at the store: tiny bunnies, eggs, or chickens. Tie these on the branches, and add ribbon bows or artificial flowers. To personalize your tree, you could ask the children to take small, colored pieces of paper, write Easter wishes or promises, fold them, and tie them to the tree.

HOLY WEEK AND EASTER

GO DUTCH

A Pennsylvania Dutch custom was to serve *red* eggs on Easter or during Holy Week. *Ahead of time*: hard-boil eggs and peel them. Drop them into the juice from a jar of pickled beets (serve the beets in a salad for supper). Add a piece of cinnamon stick and three or four cloves if you have some. Let the eggs "pickle" in the refrigerator for at least two days before serving them on a bed of shredded lettuce or just in a bowl. You might mention that the red eggs are a reminder that Jesus shed his blood for us.

SPY WEDNESDAY

The Wednesday in Holy Week was once called spy Wednesday as a reminder that this was the time when Judas plotted to betray Jesus. Tell the children this, and then take a walk and try to "spy" (observe or think of) all the things God has made: the birds and bees and trees, the flowers and rain showers, rocks and flocks of geese, clouds and rowdy little boys. You might try to make up a poem about each thing you spy.

SEE ALSO IDEAS FOR HOLY THURSDAY AND GOOD FRIDAY (SEDER SUPPER AND HOT CROSS BUNS) MENTIONED IN THE MONTH OF MARCH.

HOLY THURSDAY HAND WASHING

Establish this ritual before or after the Seder supper. Or, if you do not have a Seder, simply do this before or after your Holy Thursday family meal in remembrance of Jesus washing the feet of the apostles. Bring an empty bowl and a pitcher of lukewarm water to the table. Put a towel on your arm, and go to each person in turn. The first person puts his or her hands into the empty bowl, you pour a bit of water over his or her hands, and then dry them with the towel. Then you move on to each person present. When you are finished, you all say a brief blessing or prayer together. Make the water *scented* by adding a bit of lemon extract or perfume to make it even more special. You might alternate by having a different person do the washing each year. And it would be a good idea to have some soft religious music playing in the background to keep it solemn.

GOOD FRIDAY, GOOD GARDENERS

If you like to garden, or if you just have a small patch of flowers in your yard, you might be interested in an old custom of *blessing the garden* on Good Friday. Simply get a small container of holy water from church a few days beforehand. Take the children into the yard, and sprinkle holy water on the garden. Make up a prayer or read one from a prayer book, asking God to help the flowers or vegetables grow *and* to help your family grow in faith.

THE STATIONS OF THE CROSS

Good Friday is traditionally the day the parish has a service that includes the Stations of the Cross. But if you have small children "introduce" them to the Stations yourself. Find a quiet time on this day or any day during Lent when no one is in church. Take the children around to each station, and explain what event that station represents. Say a tiny prayer at each station like, "Dear Jesus, thank you. We love you." Since these stations or "pictures" which tell the story of the passion and death of Jesus often affect small children deeply, plan to do something together afterward. Take a walk or a drive in the country or stop at a park playground. If they want to talk about the experience, answer their questions. If they don't, just let them keep their thoughts to themselves. They may not feel like talking until some time later.

An Egg-citing Easter Project. Only God could make a chicken who could make an egg. But you can make a rubber egg! Here's how: Put an uncooked egg in the bottom of a glass. Add enough vinegar to completely cover the egg. Leave the egg in the vinegar for two days (forty-eight hours). Remove the egg from the vinegar, and gently squeeze it. It won't feel hard anymore. You will have made a "rubber" egg. How does it work? The hard eggshell is made of calcium. The acid in the vinegar dissolves the calcium leaving a soft, rubbery shell.

To advertisers and the media, Easter is a one-day happening. To Christians, Easter is a *season*, beginning with the Resurrection and ending with Pentecost, six weeks later.

Holy Water. If you don't have one now, get a small, pretty holy water fount, and put it on the wall of the children's room or any room in the house. Fill it with some of the water that was blessed on Holy Saturday. Ask the priest for some or take an empty, clean baby food jar, and fill it from the baptismal fount at church. Teach the children to use it to bless themselves with the Sign of the Cross every morning and every night. Keep it refilled through the year.

Kids Help? Sometimes it takes more time when the kids are involved. But letting kids help cook, plan, and prepare for celebrations gives them a sense of accomplishment, a sense of being a contributing part of the family. Even the youngest can pour, stir, and sprinkle. Mixing things like ordinary flour, milk, and eggs, and then watching them turn into a cake, can be an exciting thing for curious, questioning, learning children.

HOLY SATURDAY

It's time to think about Jesus rising from the dead and a good way to explain this is to tell the story of the caterpillar. Find a picture book about the caterpillar, or just talk about how a caterpillar lives in a cocoon (like Jesus stayed in the tomb for three days) and then comes out as a beautiful butterfly (the way Jesus came out of the tomb to show that we all will rise from the dead some day). To further emphasize this, serve butterfly sandwiches for lunch. It's easy to do.

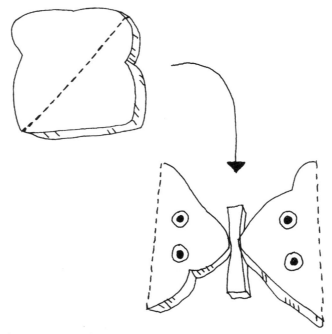

Just take a piece of white or wheat bread, cut diagonally to make two triangles, and you will have a butterfly shape. Simply spread with a flavored cheese (use the smooth kind that comes in little glasses—pimiento or whatever your children like—or make your own by mixing seasoned salt or a spice into softened cream cheese). Use a carrot stick down the middle for the "body," and add olive slices to decorate the "wings." Save the leftover triangles and spread with another soft cheese or peanut butter for finger sandwiches or dry the bread to make bread crumbs.

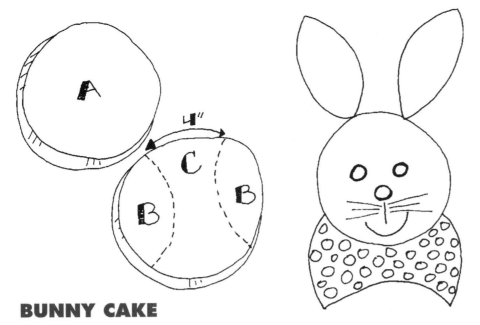

BUNNY CAKE

Kids love to have a bunny cake for Easter dessert. You can buy one but, it's very easy to make one. And if the kids help, they will enjoy it even more. Simply make two round cakes using any flavor cake mix. One cake will be the bunny head. Cut the other cake into three pieces, according to the diagram above. The two outside pieces will be the bunny ears, and the center piece will be a bunny bow tie. Assemble this cake on a cookie sheet, a large tray, or an 18- by 15-inch piece of cardboard covered with aluminum foil. Frost the cake with canned white icing, then sprinkle with flake coconut. Gently press the coconut into the icing, especially on the sides so it will stay in place. Make the bunny face using gumdrops or chocolate chips (the big chip size) for the eyes and the nose, and use red string licorice for the mouth and whiskers. If there is leftover coconut you could tint it green with a bit of food coloring and sprinkle it around the bunny for grass. Or, if your family hates coconut, you could omit that entirely and just have a white-iced bunny. Remind the children that bunnies and eggs are used to celebrate Easter because they represent the new life of springtime just as Jesus gave us all new life when he rose from the dead on Easter morning.

BUNNY BREAD

Instead of, or in addition to, the bunny cake, you can make bunny bread. Buy frozen bread dough and divide it into two parts. Shape the first half into a round shape for the bunny's body. Divide the second half into two parts. Use one part for the bunny's head. Divide the last part into two, and shape into bunny ears. Assemble on a lightly greased cookie sheet, and follow the bread package instructions for baking. Use raisins for the eyes and nose.

The Green Scene. April is the month when we celebrate Arbor Day and Earth Day. This is a good time to plant something green in your yard. If you don't have room for a tree, how about a bush or at least a few plants? Kids love digging in the dirt, so they'll be glad to help. While you're digging, challenge them to name all the different kinds of trees God made: elm, maple, cedar, oak, holly, aspen, and so on.

For a springtime cake, frost a rectangular or round cake in white icing, and then push multicolored jelly beans into the icing on the sides of the cake. Use a few jelly beans to spell out a message on the top of the cake like, "You are a great human bean!"

I Love You. Surprise the family when you are making hamburgers or sandwiches. Leave the top slice of bread off the sandwich, and use squeeze mustard or ketchup to draw a heart on the top of each hamburger or sandwich.

Notes

_____

_____

_____

_____

_____

_____

_____

_____

_____

_____

_____

_____

_____

_____

BUNNY ALTERNATE

If you are not in the mood for bunnies, make basket cupcakes. Simply top a cupcake with green icing or with white icing and green-tinted coconut. Add some jelly beans and make a "handle" for the basket with red licorice.

PROGRESSIVE DINNER

Since you will probably have Easter leftovers and your friends will too, invite them to a progressive dinner by telling them to "progress" to your house and bring their leftovers along. Maybe the kids would even like to swap leftover Easter candy. This will help with the letdown after Easter. Maybe the grownups might like to tell the children the story of "my-most-favorite-Easter when I was a child."

DO SOMEONE A FAVOR

Let the children make favors for any of your April get-togethers. For each girl (or lady), make an Easter bonnet. Simply take a paper plate, and cut a small slit on each side. Decorate the plate by gluing on artificial flowers or ribbons, or drawing on a design. Run a ribbon through the slits so the hat can be tied under the chin.

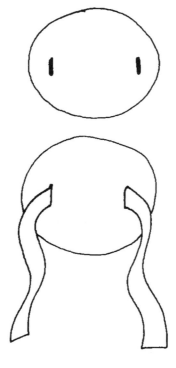

For each boy (or man), cut out the shape of a tie and decorate it with crayons and glued-on sequins or beads. Attach a piece of elastic that can slip over the neck or a piece of yarn that can be tied behind the neck.

CHICKEN PIE...FOR DESSERT?

For a really easy Easter, or after-Easter dessert, buy a package of those funny little pink or yellow marshmallow chicks (you'll need about fifteen). Put a graham cracker pie crust in a glass or microwave-safe pie plate. Fill it with a 12-ounce package of chocolate chips. Arrange the marshmallow chicks over the top of the chocolate. Microwave on high for just 20 to 30 seconds (watch carefully) or just until the chicks expand and the marshmallow starts to show through. Serve immediately while it is warm and gooey.

SEE ALSO FIRST COMMUNION IDEAS IN THE MONTH OF MAY.

MAY

MAY

Saints' Days

1	**Joseph the Worker**
2	**Athanasius**
3	**Philip and James**
12	**Nereus and Achilleus and Pancras**
14	**Matthias**
15	**Isidore the Farmer**
18	**John I**
20	**Bernardino of Siena**
25	**Bede the Venerable**
25	**Gregory VII**
25	**Mary Magdalen Dei Pazzi**
26	**Philip Neri**
27	**Augustine of Canterbury**

h, tra-la, the merry month of May and Mary, flowers and sunshine, May processions and first Communions, Mother's Day and sometimes the end of the school year.

Remember, O most gracious Virgin Mary, that never was it known that anyone who fled to your protection, implored your help, or sought your intercession was left unaided. Inspired by this confidence, I fly unto you, O virgin of virgins, my Mother. To you do I come, before you I stand, sinful and sorrowful. O Mother of the Word Incarnate, despise not my petitions but, in your mercy, hear and answer me. Amen.

MAY I ON MAY DAY?

May you celebrate on May Day? Of course! May Day has been celebrated in many places and in many ways. People celebrated the coming of summer with May poles and May processions. Workers in Europe celebrated it as a "workman's holiday." And now we honor Saint Joseph the Worker on this day. For your dinner centerpiece today why don't you have a hammer, screwdriver, nails, work gloves, or whatever you can find in your home hardware toolbox. If you have a statue of Saint Joseph, invite him to the table too. Even though Saint Joseph was probably a very "neat" worker, perhaps you could celebrate his day by serving an elegant meal of "Sloppy" Joes.

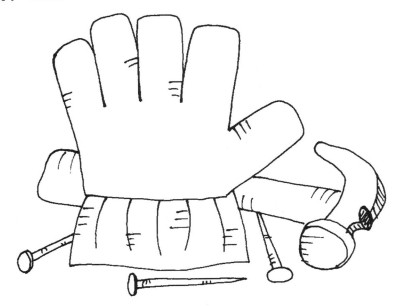

TIME TO GO A-MAYING

Celebrate this month with a simple May pole dance. Gather a lot of ribbons and some flowers. Tie ribbons in the girls' hair, and put ribbons around the boys' necks like European ties. If you have a nice tree in your backyard, go there, and if not, go to a park and find a tree in a quiet spot. Let the girls tie long ribbons around the tree, and then dance around it so the ribbons will wrap around the tree. While they're dancing they can sing a song they already know or simply chant, "Here we go a-Maying, a-Maying, a-Maying, all around the town, all around the tree." When the girls finish dancing, the boys can place flowers around the tree. Then you can all have a nice picnic in the backyard or the park. You might serve something summery like chicken salad, fruit salad, cucumber sandwiches, and iced tea. While you munch, you can talk about all the special events in May: Mother's Day, Mary's month, and Ascension Thursday.

A good marriage is like a good casserole: only those who make it know what goes into it.

Watch What You're Watching. Television viewing has become a "ritual" in some homes. Children are "born into it" and develop viewing habits in the first four to six years of life. This is why it is so important for parents to be selective and only watch morally healthy programs. Parents set the example not by what they say ("You watch too much television") but by what they do themselves.

Mail Call. During the summer, when school is out and days sometimes drag on, why not occasionally mail a note or a postcard to each child? Children love to get mail and it can be a boredom-buster summer surprise.

Half-moon Cooler. Buy a ripe honeydew melon. Cut it in half crosswise, and remove the seeds. Dissolve 2 teaspoons of unflavored gelatin in 1/2 cup boiling water. Stir in 1 cup strawberry yogurt and mix well. Stir in 1/2 cup frozen strawberries. Chill until thickened but not set. Beat with a mixer or whisk until fluffy. Spoon into the melon halves. Cover and chill for 3 hours or until firm. To serve, cut each melon half into four wedges. You will have pale green "half moons" with a pink center. This is easy but looks real fancy. While you enjoy the honeydew dessert, talk about the old honey-do jokes: Honey, do the dishes; Honey, do your homework. Ask everyone to think of honey-do jokes, and talk about how it is so much easier to get the work done if all the *honeys* in the family *do* their fair share.

THE FARMER IN THE DELL

May 15 is the feast of Saint Isidore, the farmer. So if you don't have that garden planted yet, today is the day to shovel, spade, and seed. When you get totally exhausted, you can flop on the ground and sing a few rounds of "The Farmer in the Dell."

FIRST COMMUNION TIME

April and May are the months when children usually make their first Communion. If someone in your family is making a first Communion, be sure to turn the day into a special celebration. You'll want to invite extended family and friends to come over. Use all white decorations: a white tablecloth, white flowers from the garden (or artificial white flowers), white candles, and white napkins. Tie several white balloons on the light above your table, and add lots of streamers of white ribbon. Buy some holy cards, and put one at each person's plate. You might want to use an assortment of grapes and a pretty loaf of bread as your centerpiece to symbolize the bread and wine of Eucharist. Take plenty of pictures, and have double prints made of each. You'll want to put some in your family album, of course, but also make a small album for the honoree to save as a memento. A nice gift for this occassion would be a children's Bible. Each guest could write a small note of congratulations inside the front pages of the Bible.

ASCENSION THURSDAY

The feast of the Ascension honors the day Jesus left the earth and his family and friends, and ascended into heaven. This would be a good day to buy some helium balloons. Tie one to the back of each chair at the dinner table. After dinner, take turns setting the balloons free, and watch as they "ascend." Talk to the children about this feast, and discuss how Jesus' friends must have felt when it was time for him to return to his Father in heaven. If the weather is nice, it would also be a good time to lay down in the grass and look up at the clouds and try to see who can find the most, or the most unusual or the funniest, figures in the clouds.

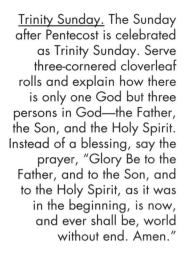

"EXPECTATION" SUNDAY

There are nine days (like a novena) between Ascension Thursday and Pentecost Sunday. The Sunday that falls in the middle of those nine days was once known as Expectation Sunday. On that day it was the custom in Mediterranean countries to drop flower petals from the ceilings of churches during Mass. Wouldn't that be fun to have flower petals falling on your head? To commemorate this day it would be nice to have a beautiful bunch of fresh flowers on your table for Sunday dinner. You could talk about the many different kinds of flowers God made and the "expectation" of watching and waiting for them to bloom in the garden each year.

Trinity Sunday. The Sunday after Pentecost is celebrated as Trinity Sunday. Serve three-cornered cloverleaf rolls and explain how there is only one God but three persons in God—the Father, the Son, and the Holy Spirit. Instead of a blessing, say the prayer, "Glory Be to the Father, and to the Son, and to the Holy Spirit, as it was in the beginning, is now, and ever shall be, world without end. Amen."

Who Is Julia Ward? In 1872, Julia Ward suggested a day should be set aside to honor mothers. But it was not until 1914 that President Woodrow Wilson signed a proclamation making the second Sunday in May Mother's Day.

Mothering Sunday. In England, Mothering Sunday was celebrated for those people who worked away from home, often as maids or butlers in castles or large homes. On this day, they would be permitted to take time off to go "a-mothering" and spend the afternoon with their mothers. And they usually took a cake along to give to mother as a gift.

May "Crowns." May processions which climax with someone placing a crown or wreath on a statue of the Blessed Mother have long been a favorite custom. If there is a May procession at your parish or at a neighboring parish, attend the celebration with the children. Afterward, they may want to make some flower crowns themselves. You can use fresh-cut flowers from the garden or artificial flowers. Use a length of florist wire long enough to wrap around the child's head plus a few extra inches to wrap together to close the circle. Then use florist tape or pipe cleaners to attach the flowers to the wire. Twist it together into a circle, and tie some ribbon streamers at the back. It would be fun to have a flower-crown, May-time breakfast party. Buy donuts or sweet rolls, and meet some friends at a park or a lake very early before anyone else is awake. The children may grumble about getting up, but once they get there you can give each of them a flower "crown," and let them frolic and munch as the sun rises. Take along a "boom box" so you can have some soft, springtime music to play as a background for the frolicking. This could become a very nice annual tradition.

MUD PIES AND DIRT CAKES FOR MOTHERS DAY?

"M" is for the many ways to celebrate this special day. The children love to get involved in preparations but you could give them a few hints. Find a recipe to make mud pie or dirt cake. They are really delicious desserts. Or you could show the children how to serve a "dirt-y" flower pot dessert. Buy enough new, small flower pots so there will be one for each person having dinner. Wash the pots and dry them thoroughly the day before. Get a package of crisp chocolate cookies (without icing), and crush them in a blender, food processor, or by hand. Working as an assembly line, put a tablespoon of crushed cookies into the bottom of each pot, fill with your favorite ice cream about three-quarters full. Top with more crushed cookies to resemble dirt. Decorate with an artificial flower growing out of the "dirt" or a paper umbrella or, if you are not squeamish, some gummy worms. And since it's Mother's Day, somebody else, not Mom, should volunteer to wash those DIRT-Y dishes.

dirt cake

20 oz. pkg chocolate sandwich cookies
8 oz. cream cheese
12 oz. whipped topping
2 (3 1/2 oz.) pkg instant vanilla pudding
1/2 stick butter
3 1/2 c. milk
1 c. powdered sugar

Crush cookies; set aside. Cream powdered sugar, butter, and cream cheese together; set aside. Mix pudding with milk, and fold in whipped topping; add cream cheese mixture, and mix together. Put 1/3 cookie crumbs in pan, pour 1/2 of the mixture over them; add 1/3 cookie crumbs, add remaining mixture. Top with remaining crumbs.
(Can put in clean flower pot and "plant" flower on top.)

MARY, MARY, NEVER CONTRARY

Since May also honors Mary, our Blessed Mother, it would be appropriate to have a statue of her with some flowers on the table on Mother's Day. Also this is a good time to start the family tradition of having a May altar.

On the first day of May, find a spot somewhere in your home for your May altar. You could use the corner of a shelf or set up a TV tray table in an out-of-the-traffic place. Put a little cloth on it—a small tablecloth, a place mat, a lacy handkerchief or whatever you have available. Center it with a statue or picture of Mary (if you don't have one, you could buy an inexpensive one at a religious goods store or a gift shop). Add a flower or plant and a candle.

Each evening in May gather the family at the May altar, light the candle, and reverently say together one Hail Mary or a decade of the rosary. If your children like to sing, they might want to sing a song to Mary or a Marian hymn. This doesn't have to be fancy or take more than a few minutes but it's a happy tradition in many Catholic homes.

GIVING MOM A HAND

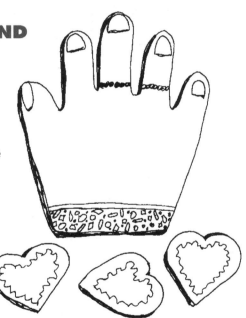

Here's another idea for this month of Mary and mothers: make heart and hand cookies. Ask each child to put his or her hand on a thin piece of cardboard (a coated paper plate is good for this also), and then trace around the hand. Cut out the hands to make patterns. Make or buy cookie dough, and roll it out on a floured board until it is about 1/4 inch thick. Place the hand patterns lightly on the dough, and use a pointed knife to carefully cut around each one. Remove the cardboard hands and the excess dough. Then, using a wide spatula, carefully place the cookies on a cookie sheet and bake. Roll out the leftover dough, and use a heart-shaped cookie cutter to cut out heart cookies. Using tubes of store-bought icing, you can decorate the hands with fingernails and rings, and "outline" the hearts. Talk to the children about how we use our hearts and our hands to love and serve God and each other.

Mother's Day Blessing. Before your meal on Mother's Day, start a motherly tradition. Suggest to the children that they make up a special Mother's Day blessing. Write out a copy for each. Ask everyone present to hold out their hands toward Mother and say the blessing together. Or say the traditional blessing before meals, and then have them hold out their hands toward Mother and simply say together, "God bless our Mother." If the children *do* compose a special blessing, save it and use it every year. (And you can do the same for Father's Day.)

Isaiah 49. "Can a mother forget her infant, be without tenderness for the child of her womb? Even should she forget, I will never forget you," says the Lord.

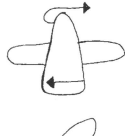

Bread Birds. Since this is the time of the year when birds are on the wing, get the children to help you make bread birds. Buy frozen bread dough, and follow the directions for preparing it but shape it this way. Divide the dough into four equal parts. On a lightly floured board, roll two parts into the shape of triangles. Roll the remaining two parts into long ovals. Twist the tops of the triangles to the right and the bottoms of the triangles to the left. Shape a beak, and add a sesame seed for the "eye." For the tail, pat the bottom part flat, and cut a few slashes to look like feathers. Do the same for the wings. Brush with beaten egg white and bake. While you are enjoying the bread birds, make a game to see who can think of the most names of the birds God made.

A FLOWERY GIFT FOR GRANDMA

Here's a gift you can help the children make for a Mother's Day present for Grandma. Get some stiff cardboard or poster board. Draw the figure of a girl about 6 1/2 inches tall (see illustration). It doesn't have to be perfect. Grandma will love it anyway. Cut out the figure and decorate it with paints or magic markers or crayons. In the center where the girl's hands would be, cut out a 3/4-inch hole. Put some water in a glass, and stand the girl against the glass. Then push the stems of a bunch of flowers through the hole in the figure and into the water in the glass. The girl will look like she is holding a bouquet of flowers!

To go along with the flower bouquet, suggest that the children also give Grandma a spiritual bouquet. Maybe you made these as a child. If not, here's how. Simply get a pretty card or piece of paper. At the top, write "Spiritual Bouquet." Then write "I promise to say one Our Father, one Hail Mary, and one Glory Be for your intention." The children can list any number of prayers as they want, but you should impress on them that they must say all the prayers they have promised. They can decorate the card with some flower drawings too.

PENTECOST SUNDAY

This is the day we celebrate the descent of the Holy Spirit upon the apostles and the "birthday" of the Catholic Church. This is the day God sent his Spirit to inspire the apostles to go out and preach and tell people about Jesus and start his Church. This would be the day to use a dove centerpiece on your Sunday dinner table. But if you don't happen to have a dove living at your house, you could "challenge" the children to make one. They could cut one out of poster board or make one out of white facial tissue. Let them loose to use their imaginations, and no matter how unusual their finished product looks, put it proudly in the middle of the table. And, since it is the birthday of the Church, maybe you could serve birthday cake for dessert.

MAMA'S IN THE KITCHEN; ALL'S RIGHT WITH THE WORLD

Little boys and little girls always remember fondly those times when they "helped" Mama bake something in the kitchen. While we're still celebrating the month of mothers, how about making some easy cupcakes. Use a grocery store mix, and bake according to the directions on the box. Then ice the cupcakes with pretty pink frosting. (Buy canned white frosting, and stir in just enough red food coloring to make a pretty pink.) Stick one pretzel stick in the top and put a candy spearmint leaf on each side of the pretzel "stem." It will just take a minute and the kids will have a memory of "cupcaking" with Mom.

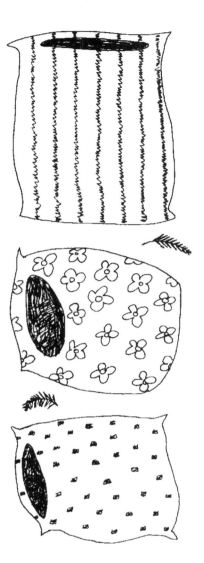

Downy Duking. If you just *have* to fight, use pillows.

MAKING MOTHER'S DAY
OR MAY-TIME RAINBOWS

Children love rainbows and this is a good month to make one at home. You will need a sunny window and a light-colored wall at a right angle to the window. Set a shallow pan of water near the window (on a table or on the window sill) so that direct sunlight falls on it. Hold a small mirror near one end of the pan. Move the mirror and the pan until they are in a spot to catch the sun, and reflect it on the wall and, presto, you will have your own private rainbow. If you move the pan closer to the wall you will get a small rainbow with bright colors. If you move it farther away from the wall you will get a bigger rainbow with paler colors. Talk about the way God puts a rainbow in the sky to cheer you after a rainstorm, and suggest that you have made a rainbow in your home to cheer everyone on this happy May day.

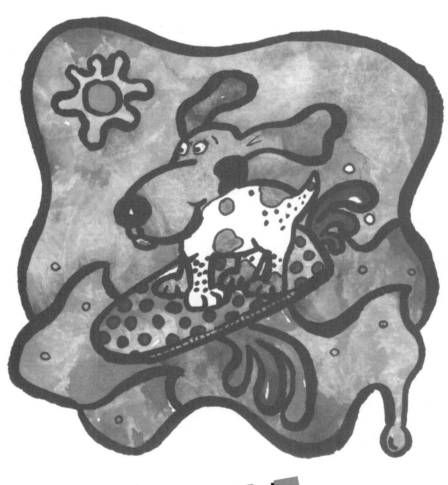

JUNE

JUNE

Saints' Days

1 **Justin Martyr**
2 **Marcellinus**
3 **Charles Lwanga and Companions**
5 **Boniface**
6 **Norbert**
9 **Ephraem the Syrian**
11 **Barnabus**
13 **Anthony of Padua**
19 **Romuald**
21 **Aloysius Gonzaga**
22 **Paulinus of Nola**
22 **John Fisher and Thomas More**
24 **The Birth of John the Baptist**
27 **Cyril of Alexander**
28 **Irenaeus of Lyons**
29 **Peter and Paul**

 une, moon, balloon, and happy tunes for the June brides, graduates, and honored Dads on Father's Day. It's summertime, vacation time, lazy, hazy days time… and, as usual, celebration time.

He was but as the cuckoo is in June,
Heard, not regarded.

Shakespeare

Such bounty God gives us in this lush, ripe month. We hurry along, not glorying in the flowers on the path, not listening to the bird on the wing. All too often God's creations and mercies are seen and heard, but not regarded.

TAKE THIS RING

June is often wedding month, and children love the festivities before and after a wedding. When there's a wedding in your family, let the children help with the preparations, and talk to them about your own wedding and their grandparents' weddings so they'll grow up knowing that a wedding is a special (and holy) occasion.

HOORAY FOR DAD

Faster than a speeding toddler, able to change diapers in a single bound, master plumber, auto repairer, house fixer-upper, and great storyteller: it's Super Dad! And it's time to celebrate *his day*. Did you know that the United States is one of the few countries where a day is set aside to officially honor fathers? The idea was first promoted by Mrs. John Dodd of Spokane, Washington. After her mother died at an early age, her father raised six children by himself, so Mrs. Dodd thought he and other fathers like him deserved a day of honor. Father's Day was first celebrated in the early 1900s. In 1916 Woodrow Wilson participated in the celebration, but it was not made a national holiday until 1972. Today, the third Sunday in June is observed each year as a special time to give recognition and appreciation to fathers. Of course, the best way to start the day is to go to church as a family to honor God the Father.

The children may want to make a special Father's Day card. Suggest they use a picture of Saint Joseph plus some items that indicate Dad's hobbies: golf tees, a baseball, a hammer or wrench, and/or use some of these items for your dinner centerpiece. If the children have used their allowance to buy a gift, you can suggest they wrap it in some unusual way. They could wrap it in the sports page of the newspaper, in a pennant of Dad's favorite team, or a road map and use ribbon to tie on a tire gauge.

Chore Change. Suggest that the family *exchange chores* for a day or a week to find out what it's like to *walk in someone else's shoes.*

Rice Is Nice. Did you know that rice has been grown and eaten since ancient times? Historians in India and China have traced it as far back as 3,000 years B.C. (before Christ). But it was not grown in the United States until the end of the seventeenth century. Get takeout Chinese food *with rice* for dinner. Talk about how the country of China is so different from our country, but how God watches over the people in *all* countries.

Tic Toc Tic Toc. Ten minutes is too short if it's recess but too long if you're being punished.

Edible Cups. Buy the kind of ice-cream cones that have flat bottoms (so you can sit them down), and use them to serve summertime snacks for the kids to take on the run. Fill them with candies, grapes, jelly beans, popcorn, or even carrot sticks. And, if you want to, use them for ice cream too. Put a marshmallow in the bottom of the cup first and it won't get drippy as fast.

The Garden Variety.

- "Gardens are not made by sitting in the shade."

  Rudyard Kipling

- "God Almighty first planted a garden."

  Francis Bacon

- "Adam was a gardener, And God, who made him, sees

  That half of all good gardening

  Is done upon the knees."

  Rudyard Kipling

- "When the root is deep, there is no reason to fear the wind." This is true with families.

  Chinese Proverb

- It is important to give your children roots *before* you give them wings.

- All gardens have weeds and all families do too. But sometimes weeds are persistent survivors. And sometimes "weedy" relatives turn out just fine.

FOR THE "SHOWER POWER" DAD

The children might like to *make* a card or gift. Here's a simple idea for a homemade gift (which may or may not delight Dad but will give the kids something to do)—Dad's very own soap on a rope. Grate one (3 1/2 ounce) bar of plain white soap onto waxed paper. Mix 3 tablespoons of water with 1 or 2 drops of food coloring in a saucepan, and bring to a boil. Add the grated soap and reduce the heat. Stir rapidly for 2 minutes until all the shavings are colored. Remove from heat and wait until it's cool enough to handle but still warm. Carefully shape the warm mixture into three balls, inserting a length of cotton roping (bought at a fabric store) into each one to form a loop long enough to go around Dad's neck. Let cool completely, and then store in plastic wrap. Just wait till Dad tells his friends he has homemade soap on a rope!

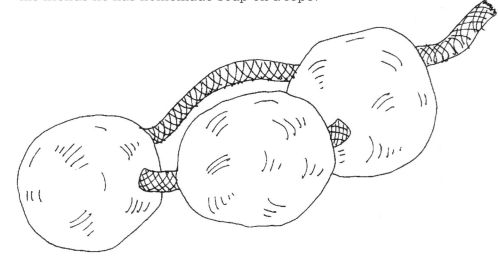

FOR THE LET'S-DO-SOMETHING DAD

If Dad likes to be on the go, this could be a good day to take a walk in the woods and look for "treasures" put there by our Heavenly Father: acorns, berries, birds, squirrels, rabbits, plants, flowers. Or you could go to a park and take along a trash bag and disposable plastic gloves. Picking up trash may not seem like a way to celebrate, but it would be a good family activity to make everyone feel good about saving the environment.

GRADUATION AND WEDDING GIFTS

Yes, this is the month for events that include gift giving so consider giving a religious item: a crucifix, statue, prayer book, Bible, or holy water fount. Since people usually receive material gifts, this would be a thoughtful way to add a spiritual significance to the "new life" beginning for either a graduate or a newlywed couple.

ANNIVERSARY TIME, TOO

Since this is the month for weddings, it's also a popular month for anniversaries. It's important to celebrate *every* anniversary because it's another happy plateau achieved. On special anniversaries, the tenth, twenty-fifth, fiftieth, some people invite in friends and family and ask a priest to celebrate Mass in their home. They might also choose to renew their marriage vows during the service. If there's an anniversary in your family, consider having a home Mass and then a little reception afterwards—even if it's just punch and cookies.

SMILE FOR THE BIRDIE!

Try to take a family photo on every anniversary. Also make it a family ritual to look through your wedding album on every anniversary, and talk about all the things that have happened since "way back when."

RALLY 'ROUND THE FLAG

June 14 is celebrated as Flag Day. Teach the children to be proud of their country—as well as their Church—and to treat the flag with respect. If you have a big flag, be sure to display it. If you don't, get some small flags, and tie a bunch to your mailbox or put some in an outdoor flower pot. For a Flag Day red-white-and-blue dessert, buy a cherry pie, and top each piece with a big scoop of vanilla ice cream and then a spoonful of canned blueberry pie filling.

Do You Believe in Tooth Fairies? If you plan to pass out quarters for each lost tooth, you might want to make "magic" quarters. Just spray a bit of hair spray on the quarter and then sprinkle it with gold glitter. You could also sprinkle a bit of the glitter on the pillow when you leave the quarter.

Kid's Kitchen Rules.
#1. Before you start to cook, wash your hands.
#2. Wearing an apron will help you keep your clothes clean.
#3. Read, or let Mom read, the directions and get out all the ingredients and all the tools you will need.
#4. Put all the ingredients on a tray, and then set each one off the tray as you use it. This way you won't forget what you've put in the recipe, and you won't leave anything out.
#5. When you finish, clean up the kitchen.
#6. Have fun.

Un-hurried Hugs. When you've had a busy day, don't feel guilty about serving a hurry-up meal so you'll have the time and energy to cuddle and read a bedtime story to the children. The cuddle will be remembered. The dinner will be forgotten.

Bar-b-har-har. June is barbecue time and a good opportunity to have a rib tickling night. For dinner, barbecue on your grill or buy some takeout from a good rib restaurant. While you are gnawing on the bones, tell this Father Schultz story. "The secret of saintliness is to develop your bones. First your head bone: you've got to think before you act. Next your backbone: you've got to have the backbone to stand up for what you believe. Then the knee bone: never forget the importance of prayer. And finally, the funny bone: you've got to be able to laugh at yourself."

A Card for Pop. Suggest to the kids that they make a Father's Day card that says "A Card for My Pop." Then draw pictures of a POPsickle, a bowl of POPcorn, a picture of POP art, a can of soda POP.

A Riddle for Pop. What do you call a sleeping bull? A bulldozer.

SCHOOL'S OUT SO WHAT DO WE DO NOW?

Try log rolling. Go to a park and find a grassy hill. Then have the kids (and Mom and Dad) lie on their sides and roll sideways down the hill. Climbing back up is good exercise. Though all of this sounds silly, it's really lots of fun. Or try kangaroo hopping. Everyone has to hop like a kangaroo, and then the leader calls out orders to hop forward, backward, sideways, or around in a circle. While you catch your breath, someone else can take a turn being the leader. This is not a "spiritual" activity, but doing fun things together makes memories and forms bonds that are not material...so they must be spiritual. But you could also stop by the church on your way home and make a visit together as a family and light a candle. If you go at a time when the church is quiet and you have it all to yourselves, it can create a time of peace and togetherness. And you might need that after all the rolling and hopping.

BE A WEATHER FORECASTER

Help the children make a weather chart, listing the days of the week and the possible weather: cloudy, rainy, sunny, windy, or stormy. Each night for a week, each child checks off what he or she thinks the weather will be the next day. Each day you put a gold star or a sticker on the one who was right. At the end of the week, you can see who guessed what kind of weather God was going to provide. You might go to the library and check out a book about weather and learn about all the different kinds of clouds that God makes.

LET'S GO FISHING!

June 29 is the feast of Saint Peter who was a fisherman and Saint Paul who helped Peter "fish" for souls. Celebrate by taking the kids on a fishing trip or going to a restaurant for a fish dinner. Be sure to talk about the fact that you are doing this to honor the feast day of the apostles. Discuss how you could each start to "fish" by telling others about your faith and trying to bring others closer to God and the Church.

NOT SPRING BUT SUMMER CLEANING

Summer is supposed to be a lazy time so announce to the kids that it is time for a ONE-ON-ONE. Tell them it is cleaning day but they will just clean out one closet or one drawer or one room. Let them each choose which they will do. Then see who can get finished first while still doing a thorough job.

Have a large garbage bag on hand, and let each make donations of any no-longer-wanted clothing or toys. When all are finished, go out for an ice-cream cone, and drop off the donation bag at some charitable drop-off box. You could make this a monthly summer activity and possibly get some cleaning done, plus help out a charity!

AND THE WINNER IS...

Start your own award program. Instead of an Oscar or an Emmy, name it something appropriate for your family—the Smithy, the Jonesy, the Whoopie or whatever. Make the awards look like blue ribbons by using leftover seals or stickers and ribbon with a safety pin on the back. The kids could help you make the awards, but the parents will decide who receives the award each week. Present the award at your weekly Sunday dinner gathering, and everyone can guess who will get it each week. Award it for a different category each time, and make the categories a surprise, sometimes funny, sometimes serious: For the one with the smelliest socks this week; for the one who was most attentive at Mass this week; for the one who ate the most meatloaf this week; for the one who taught us a good lesson this week; for the one who did the kindest act this week. Just do this for a few weeks and stop. Then revive it a few weeks later, and then stop it again, and so on as long as it works. If you make it "special" and fun, the kids might even collect those awards to see who can get the most.

Christmas in June? June 24 is one of the oldest Church feasts: a celebration of the birthday of Saint John the Baptist. It was once called "summer Christmas," and great bonfires were lit to honor the saint who was a bright, burning light; the saint who announced to the world that Jesus was coming and who constantly preached and prepared the way for Jesus, the light of the world. It was also the custom to have great picnics around the bonfire, so why not have a picnic around your outdoor grill or around a grill in a park. Pass around a portable tape recorder, and let each one "announce" why or how he or she has been blessed. Then join hands to say the traditional meal blessing.

A Sweet-n-Sour Idea. When lemons are on sale, buy a bag full. Squeeze out the juice, remove the seeds, and pour the juice into ice cube trays. Freeze, remove from trays, and then store the cubes in a plastic bag in the freezer. You'll have them handy to use in recipes that call for fresh lemon juice or ready to make a tall cool pitcher of lemonade for your picnic.

VACATION TIME

If you're planning a vacation this year, let the children help you look at maps and make plans. And when you are traveling, always check to see where there is a Catholic church so you can celebrate at Mass on Sunday. You can't teach the children the value of *always going to church* on Sunday if you let yourself skip whenever getting there is inconvenient. And besides, it's interesting to see different churches and meet new people in new parishes.

VACATIONING AT HOME

If you can't vacation out of town this year, help the children collect maps of places they would like to go "some day." Then explore your own town. Spend a day in a neighborhood you've never visited before. Have lunch at a restaurant there, look in the shops, and pretend you are in a new town. On Sunday, continue your "vacation" by going to Mass in a church you've never visited before, and then have breakfast or lunch in a nearby restaurant. During the meal, talk about what was different and what was the same in this church compared to *your own* parish church—the music, the statues, the homily.

TIME FOR A HALF BIRTHDAY!

Sometimes a birthday falls at the wrong time of the year, a time when it is hard to celebrate because of bad weather or being too near Christmas or New Year's. If someone in your family had a December birthday and didn't like it, give them a half-birthday party in June—exactly six months or half a year later. Serve half a cake or a cake that is half vanilla, half chocolate. Serve half sandwiches, half a glass of punch, half a bowl of nuts. Gag gifts could be one glove or one sock (half a pair!), half a box of candy, and you could sing half a song. If someone has a summer birthday when everyone is on vacation, repeat this half party idea next winter.

JULY

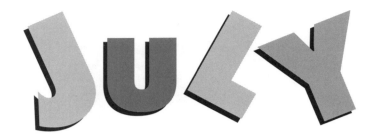

JULY

Saints' Days

1 **Blessed Junipero Serra**
3 **Thomas**
4 **Elizabeth of Portugal**
5 **Anthony Zaccaria**
6 **Maria Goretti**
11 **Benedict of Nursia**
13 **Henry II**
14 **Blessed Kateri Tekakwitha**
14 **Camillus of Lellis**
15 **Bonaventure**
16 **Our Lady of Mount Carmel**
21 **Lawrence of Brindisi**
22 **Mary Magdalene**
23 **Bridget of Sweden**
25 **James the Great**
26 **Joachim and Anne**
29 **Martha**
30 **Peter Chrysologus**
31 **Ignatius of Loyola**

Oh, say can you see all the possibilities for celebrations this month? Of course there's the Fourth of July and the freedom of summertime but also several special saint days.

America, America.
Red, white, and blue doth wave
To signal for the world to see
The home of free and brave.

GO FORTH ON THE FOURTH

Strike up the band! Here comes a parade! On this hooray-for-America day, start out by attending an early Mass to give thanks for this wonderful country. Then how about getting the neighborhood kids and parents to have a bicycle parade. Plan ahead by discussing the idea with other parents and choosing a starting time. The kids can have a lot of fun decorating their bicycles and tricycles with red, white, and blue streamers, balloons, ribbons. They could even make some star-spangled cardboard license plates for each "vehicle." To add "engine" noise, you can use clothes pins to attach playing cards to the spokes of the bicycle wheels and have plenty of vrrrummm vrrrummm sounds.

But wait! You can't have a parade without music. Someone could carry along a tape recorder playing patriotic music, but it would be fun to add some homemade musical instruments too, especially for the little ones. And what better instrument than an old pan you can beat with a spoon or a bunch of metal measuring spoons that can be jiggled together for a tinkling sound. An empty oatmeal box or an empty coffee can make a good tom-tom drum. And a tambourine is easy to make. Just put some uncooked macaroni or dry beans between two paper plates and staple the plates together. Decorate with ribbons or crayon drawings. End the parade by everyone singing "God Bless America."

Knock, knock. Who's there? Tarzan. Tarzan who? Tarzan stripes forever! Happy Fourth of July.

<u>Prime Picks.</u> If you have a garden, pick flowers before ten o'clock in the morning while they are still fresh from the night. If you pick them later they will wilt faster. To keep them fresh longer, add a bit of plant food to the water in the vase.

<u>Hidden Talent.</u> If your children have a special talent in sports, music, or art, help them to cultivate it. But don't let them focus on that talent alone. Teach them to keep a balance by encouraging them to try new things. They may have even greater hidden talents that have not been discovered. And *you* may too.

Things are never as bad as they seem at first. Don't panic. Everything usually looks better in the morning.

Pay attention to small things. Be alert to notice problems while they are still small. It's much harder to solve them if you keep putting them off until they become big problems.

When you *keep score* in a family, nobody wins.

A Colorful Way to Save Money. Buy a lot of colorful wash cloths when they're on sale, and use them instead of paper napkins for family meals and casual entertaining. They're easy to toss in the wash and much less expensive than paper products. And they're kinda fun too.

Have a Box Lunch. Kids love boxes. They like to make playhouses out of refrigerator boxes, but you don't have too many of those in a lifetime. Instead, save large packing boxes when something is shipped to your house. And when you have enough, label each box with a child's name. Turn it on its side so that the open flaps will make "doors" and the kids can crawl inside. Announce that you are having a box lunch. Then serve sandwiches on paper plates and drinks in paper cups to each kid in his or her own "box seat."

HOORAY FOR THE RED, WHITE, AND BLUE

For an easy Fourth of July centerpiece, make firecrackers. Ahead of time, when you use up rolls of paper towels or foil, save the empty cardboard tubes. Then cover each tube with red paper, tucking in the ends, and glue a string "fuse" on one end. You could add red and white flowers in a blue vase or just a container filled with small American flags. For an easy Fourth of July dessert, make or buy a 12- by 8-inch cake, and frost with white icing or white whipped topping. Make a flag by using halved strawberries for the stripes and a corner of blueberry stars. (See illustration.)

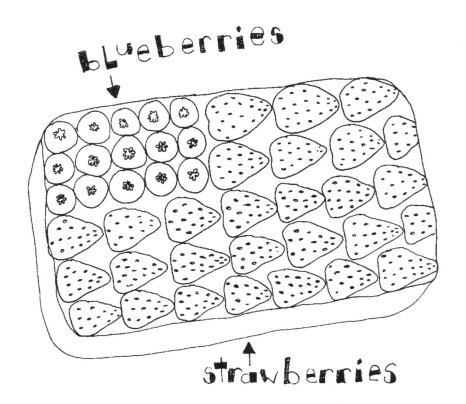

For an even easier dessert, serve a bowl of strawberries and blueberries, topped with white whipped topping.

For a little-harder-but-still-easy dessert, make a Miss American pie. Fill a baked 10-inch pie crust with a can of blueberry pie filling. Chill 30 minutes. Beat a softened 8-ounce package of cream cheese with 1 cup of sifted confectioner's sugar until smooth. Fold in one 12-ounce container of whipped topping. Spread on top of blueberry filling. Chill another 30 minutes. Gently spread a can of cherry pie filling on top. And there you have a red, white and blue pie. Whichever dessert you choose, always serve the same on the Fourth of July to make it a tradition.

DO ME ANOTHER FAVOR?

Since kids love to make favors, they might like to make Uncle Sam hats to use as favors for July gatherings. It's easy to do. Buy red and white striped paper cups. Cut out circles of blue construction paper (about 4 inches in diameter), and glue the bottom, closed end of a cup onto each blue circle. Cut small strips of the blue paper (about 1 inch by 7 inches). Add silver stars to each strip, and glue one strip around each cup to make a hat band. Turn up two opposite sides of the blue circles to make the hat brims. Fill the cups with candy sticks or small wrapped candies. (See illustration.)

ON THE EVE OF THE FOURTH

July 3 is the feast of Saint Thomas. Get out the Bible, and read or tell the story of "doubting" Thomas. Discuss how it was a very unusual thing for Jesus to rise from the dead so Thomas might be excused for doubting—just like we sometimes doubt something that Mommy or Daddy tells us. But as soon as Thomas saw the truth, saw Jesus' hands, he did believe and from then on he never doubted again. Talk about how we must always tell the truth, as Jesus did, so that others will know they can always believe us. Explain how many of the things Catholics believe are contained in the words of the Apostles' Creed. Join hands and say the Apostles' Creed together. If the children don't know the words, this would be a good time to start teaching this prayer and a good time for parents to think again about all the things this prayer means.

HAVE A POCKET NIGHT

Serve pita bread sandwiches tonight, and tell the kids you're having pockets for supper. Have several ingredients (meat, cheese, lettuce, tomatoes), and let each decide what to stuff into the pocket. While you're munching, explain that pita is very similar to the big, flat breads that the people from Middle Eastern cultures make in fire ovens and that this kind of bread probably dates back to biblical times. So just *maybe* Jesus once had a pocket sandwich

Leaf It to Me. With all the trees in full leaf, this would be a good month to encourage the children to make a leaf collection, trying to find as many different leaves as possible. Then you can have a round-leaf discussion about how they are all similar but different and how God made them (and us) that way.

Spaghetti Cake? When frosting a cake, do you ever have trouble with the layers slipping and sliding? If you do, when you add the top layer, stick long pieces of thin uncooked spaghetti down through the center of all layers, and then continue frosting. As the frosting hardens, carefully remove the spaghetti and no one will know the difference.

Oui Oui. The French have the expression, *cuisine de tendresse.* There is no exact English translation but it means that when food is prepared and served with traditions of faith and family, it is a wonderful gift. Try to make as many meals as possible *family* meals. Sharing food leads to sharing confidences and fun.

Always be ready to share credit as well as blame.

The Name Game. If someone in the family has achieved something special like doing extra chores or cutting the grass without complaining, honor him or her with a name night. For dinner, serve only things that start with the first letter of the honoree's name. If the name is **A**nn, serve **A**pple salad (chopped apples, raisins, and nuts mixed with mayonnaise), or **A**rtichoke salad (simply add a jar of marinated artichokes to a green salad), or **A**ngel hair pasta with your favorite sauce, and **A**ngel food cake with ice cream for dessert. If the name is **B**ill, serve **B**urgers, **B**aked **B**eans, **B**read and **B**utter, and **B**rownies for dessert. You get the idea. This could be a year-round tradition that could lead to some very unusual dinners.

During dinner, you can talk about how special a person's name is, especially if it's a saint's name. Then everyone could tell why they like or don't like the name they have and how they might like to change it. You can also discuss what each of you could do to "make a name for yourself."

too! Talk about how God gives us lots of pockets because each day is like a pocket: some days we stuff treasures into our pockets and other days there is only lint! After dinner, the family could sit in a circle and take turns emptying pockets (and maybe Mom could empty her purse) to see what different kinds of "treasures" each has. Then you could consider what has happened that day that you consider a treasure and what has happened that you consider lint. Join hands and say a prayer that you will treasure each day and try to stuff only good things into your pockets. Pocket night could become a once-a-month tradition.

A DAY TO CELEBRATE GRANDPARENTS

July 26 is the feast day of Saint Joachim and Saint Anne, the parents of Mary, our Blessed Mother. So you might think of these saints as Jesus' grandparents. Celebrate this day by inviting the grandparents to dinner and maybe having the children make them little presents or favors for the table. Or, if the grandparents live out of town, help the children make cards or write letters or call them on the phone. During dinner, talk about how Jesus might have spent an "overnight" with his grandparents or might have gone to visit them and had dinner at their house. Talk about how maybe these saints were once babysitters for Jesus. Celebrate this day in some special way to honor the grandparents every year.

WHILE WE'RE ON THE "GRAND" SUBJECT

Once upon a time, extended families sat around telling stories of "way back when." Today, with such busy lives, television to watch, and computer games to play, there's less story telling. But some day, children will be sorry they don't know much about their grandparents' "former" lives. On the next birthday, "gift" the grandparents with a small tape recorder and some tapes (or even a camcorder and tapes), and ask them to start recording little memories from their lives. Ask them to tell stories of how the world was when they were children, of wedding days and baptism days, of how birthdays were celebrated, of how Christmas was observed, of how food was prepared differently, of how transportation was different, and also of how the Church was different. Every so often, plan a "grand" evening to listen to the tapes together.

MONEY, MONEY, MONEY

When it's time to give your child an allowance, along with the money, also give the child a small bank or a jar with the label "Happy Jar" or "The Giving Jar." Explain that God has given us so many good things, we should return the favor by giving to others. Explain that each time the child spends a dollar, he or she should put a dime (or more) in the jar. If you have several children, they might compare to see who is being careful to add to the giving fund. When enough has been collected, you can have a family discussion about how to use it—put it in the collection basket, send it to a charity. This can make tithing a happy habit instead of a chore.

MORE MONEY MATTERS

When it's housecleaning time, help your little helper look forward to the weekly chore. Hide a few nickels or dimes in places that need to be dusted or vacuumed. This turns the chore into an adventure, a treasure hunt. It won't cost much and it will reward you both— the child gets the coins and you get the job done with less complaining.

A MYSTERY TOUR

To some children, the church is a mystery. They don't understand the idea of holy water, genuflection, and other symbols. Some sunny afternoon, take the children into the quiet, dark, cool church for a tour. Explain that when we dip our fingers in the holy water, we "bless ourselves" (make the Sign of the Cross) because we are entering a very special place, God's house, and the holy water reminds us of our baptism. If they don't know how, show them how to reverently bless themselves. Explain that we genuflect because we are "bowing down" to say hello to God and to show that we honor God. If there are statues, explain who they represent and how we have statues in church the same way we have photos of our ancestors in a photo album: to honor and to remember them. You might even take them up to the altar and let them touch it reverently. Explain that this special table is a very holy place where the priest celebrates Mass and changes bread and wine into the body and blood of Jesus (just like Jesus did at the Last Supper) because the priests are the followers of the apostles and Jesus chose them to do his work on earth when he went back to heaven. Once children understand the church, hopefully they will be more reverent and quiet and respectful during Mass.

Spending *money* on someone can never take the place of spending *time*.

Smile! If the summer days are beginning to drag, go somewhere that has one of those 4-for-$1 photo booths. Let the kids take turns posing alone or together. You'll get more than a dollar's worth of fun.

Founding Father Riddle. What did Benjamin Franklin say when he discovered electricity? Nothing. He was too shocked!

Revolutionary Father Riddle. What did they wear at the Boston Tea Party? Tea Shirts!

Traditions Count. "A happy childhood carries its own brightness to another generation, springing up with glad anticipations and bright recollections." Godey's Lady's Book, 1856

FRISBEE FUN TIME

In this great outdoor month, it's a good time to have a Frisbee afternoon. Did you know that Frisbee fun began back in the 1920s when college kids found out it was fun to throw metal pie tins? Those tins were made by the Frisbie Baking Company. In 1957, the Wham-O Company introduced a flying disk but first named it the Pluto Platter because people then were fascinated by the idea of UFOs that came from a faraway planet. Since then more than one hundred million Frisbee disks have been sold. You probably have at least one but, if you don't, they're inexpensive to buy. The kids might like to invite a friend or two or maybe a dog or two, since dogs love to play Frisbee too. After the fun, you can serve small individual pizzas that look like Frisbees. And you can talk about how God's love is like a Frisbee: a circle with no beginning and no end. Suggest that God must love round things since he made the world round. Have a game to name all the round things that are good: cakes, pies, baseballs, basketballs, the sun, the moon, some flowers, some heads. And don't forget halos!

TIME TO TEACH THE THUMB PRAYER

Long ago, parents taught their children to "pray with the thumb!" In the warm summer days of July, children play hard and are so tired at night they are sometimes too sleepy to say bedtime prayers. So this is a good time to teach them to simply use their thumb to make the Sign of the Cross on their forehead or over their heart, over and over, until they fall asleep. You might also teach them that when they get restless during Mass, they can "thumb" the Sign of the Cross on the palm of their hand while they think of Jesus. This is a good, quiet, meditative prayer.

AUGUST

Saints' Days

1 **Alphonsus Liguori**
2 **Eusebius of Vercelli**
4 **John Vianney**
7 **Sixtus II and Companion**
7 **Cajetan**
8 **Dominic de Guzman**
10 **Lawrence**
11 **Clare of Assisi**
13 **Pontian and Hippolytus**
14 **Maximilian Kolbe**
16 **Stephen of Hungary**
19 **John Eudes**
20 **Bernard of Clairvaux**
21 **Pius X**
23 **Rose of Lima**
24 **Bartholomew**
25 **Louis IX**
27 **Monica**
28 **Augustine**
29 **Beheading of John the Baptist**

The word August means stately, magnificent, exalted. Could this be because there are so many saints' days this month? Since this is the last summer month before school begins and life gets serious, make the most of it.

Things turn out best for people who make the best of the way things turn out.

— **Art Linkletter** —

AUGUST 1 IS FOR ALPHONSUS

The first day of August is the feast of Saint Alphonsus Liguori, the patron saint of writers. Celebrate by going on a field trip to the library. Let the children bring home a wagonload of books. You can spend the week reading to each other. With a book, you can travel together to merry old England for a cup of tea, visit the Great Wall of China, watch the sun set over the ocean, sip hot chocolate as you watch snow fall on the Alps, or spend the afternoon with Dr. Seuss. What a way to celebrate! You can also tell the children that Saint Alphonsus got a college degree and became a lawyer when he was sixteen years old! If you ask what they plan to do when they are sixteen, they'll probably answer, "Get a driver's license." Saint Alphonsus later became a priest, a prolific writer, and founder of the Redemptorists, a religious order of missionaries, writers, extraordinary preachers, and pastors.

THE DOG DAYS OF AUGUST

August is known for its hot and steamy "dog days," once believed to be an evil time "when the sea boiled, wine turned sour, dogs grew mad, and all creatures became languid, causing people burning fevers, hysterics and phrensies" (from *Brady's Clavis Calendarium*, 1813).

Sounds like it's time to have a hot dog party. If you're brave, invite the kids' friends to bring along their dogs (the kids would love that), and then decorate the dogs with paper party hats, ribbons on their collars, bandanas, and have a pet parade.

With or without the four-legged dogs, be sure to serve grilled hot dogs. To give them an extra zip, make them into "Coney Island" hot dogs. Just heat up a can of chili, and add a bit of that to each bun plus some chopped onion, pickle relish, and grated cheese. When you say the blessing, let each kid say a special prayer for his or her favorite puppy dog.

Believing and Knowing. "Understanding is the reward of faith. Therefore seek not to understand that thou may believe, but believe that thou may understand." Saint Augustine

No Artificial Turf. As summer winds down, boredom sets in. Try planting a sponge garden. Soak a sponge in water, and place it in a shallow dish. Sprinkle it with grass seed. Keep the sponge moist, and let the kids keep track of how many days it takes to grow "an indoor lawn."

If All Else Fails. Give each kid a squirt gun, and turn them loose in the backyard. Then get inside and lock the door! And the next time you have an adult backyard party, pass out squirt guns to them too, and see how much fun you can have when silly grownups get a squirt gun in their hands.

"A smile is a curve that sets everything straight." Phyllis Diller

Plan Ahead. If there's a baby in the family, keep a small diaper bag packed and ready to go to Sunday Mass. Then, in the confusion of everyone getting ready, all you'll have to add is a bottle. For older children, keep a *church bag* packed with small toys, religious books, and maybe a holy card or a small plastic statue or a wooden rosary. Put things in the bag that they will not play with during the week but are special for Sunday. And maybe let them add one favorite take-along each week.

Adventure This Month. If your kids like only rock music, take them to a symphony. Some cities have special "kids' days" at the symphony. Or introduce them to classical music by borrowing some tapes or CDs from a friend or checking some out at the public library. And how about trying some religious music? You can buy or borrow beautiful classical religious music, gospel songs, or chant.

RECONCILIATION

August 4 is the feast of Saint John Vianney, a priest and confessor who sometimes spent sixteen hours a day in the confessional, reconciling people with God! Honor his feast day by gathering the family and going to church on Saturday to receive the sacrament of reconciliation. Be sure to check first to see what time confession is available. Pray that God will help you become reconciled with your lot, your life, and God's plan for you.

MAKING CHANGES

August 6 is the feast of the Transfiguration of the Lord; a day to do some serious thinking. Consider how you could "transfigure" yourself and your family: spend more time playing games together and less time watching television; work an exercise plan into your busy schedule; use a few minutes each day to read the Bible; find a way to put more fun into your everyday life!

A "PATRON" SAINT FOR TELEVISION?

Yep! That would be Saint Clare of Assisi whose feast is August 11. Resolve this day to be more careful to monitor the programs your children watch and to be brave enough to point out to them when something on television is funny or cute but *not* Christian. Help them to become discriminating viewers.

TIME FOR A BOXING MATCH

If you have some of those boxes left from last month's box lunch, get them out. If not, stop by the grocery store and ask for some empty boxes. Challenge the kids to see who can make something interesting. Suggestions: If you have a large box, you can cut a round hole in one side, then hang a foil pie pan, attached by a string and a sturdy knot to the top edge of the hole, so that the pan swings freely in the center. Then throw tennis balls at the target. Or open a lemonade stand using a sturdy box as the table, or use a folding table for that and use the box for the "cashier's" stand. Or make a castle. Cut notches along the top of the box for the castle wall, and cut a door near the bottom that opens *down* like a drawbridge. The kids will think of a lot more ideas. When playtime is over, serve a snack and say a prayer to thank God for giving us imagination.

COLLEGE TACKLE?

If someone in your family or a friend's family is going off to college this year, give them a special present. Buy a small fishing tackle box or tool box, and fill it with things they might need but not think to take: a small hammer, screwdriver, nails, tape, small sewing kit, paper clips, rubber bands, stamps, envelopes, a few quarters to use in a coin laundry, and so on. Also

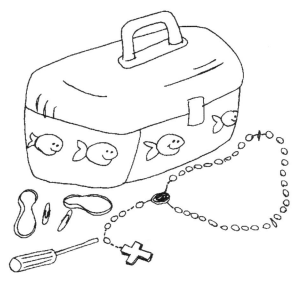

include a rosary, a small prayer book, and maybe a little statue of Mary or Joseph as a subtle reminder to take along their religion. Kids who've received a gift like this have said they couldn't believe how often they "tackled the box" and how often it had just what they needed.

MARY'S EASTER

August 15 is sometimes called "Our Lady's Easter" because it is the feast of the Assumption, the day we believe Mary went to join her son in heaven. It was once the custom to decorate the church and the home with fragrant bouquets of herbs on this day. To keep this custom, you might buy some small pots of herbs at the grocery store, and put these in a basket for your centerpiece at dinnertime. If there is mint growing in your yard or in a friend's yard, serve iced tea with sprigs of fresh mint in it.

This would be a good day to start a family ritual of saying at least one decade of the rosary each week together as a family. Look at your calendar and find the most likely day, and ask the family to agree to try to gather at that same time each week for a tribute to Mary.

To get the children into the mood of the feast, you might suggest that everyone wear something blue this day. If they agree, you could do this every year and make your own family tradition—the same way people always wear something green on Saint Patrick's Day.

Doggone Good. In these "dog days" of August, think of the story about the man whose dog was always so happy to see him—jumping, barking, wagging his tail. The man said his one prayer was, "Dear Lord, please make me as good as my dog THINKS I am."

Question: What kind of shoes are made from banana skins?

Answer: Slippers.

Serve banana splits for a cool snack or dessert today.

A Meal You Can Bet On. Jemmy Twitcher, otherwise known as John Montagu, Fourth Earl of Sandwich, was a notorious gambler as well as an aristocrat and a member in good standing at the court of King George III of England. During one of his twenty-four hour gambling marathons, he didn't want to stop to eat so he grabbed a hunk of meat and slapped it between two slabs of bread. And the sandwich was invented!

August is National Sandwich Month. So be a *hero* to someone this month. Rent a *submarine* movie video. Join a little theater group and be a *ham.* Say *cheese* and take some family pictures. And remember which side your *bread* is buttered on.

Good Giving. Definition of buckshot: a dollar spent the wrong way.

When you make out your budget, always remember to include a weekly donation for your parish (someone has to pay those heat, light, and upkeep bills), and try to add a bit extra for some charity.

"Hear the other side."
Saint Augustine

Bowl of Fortune. On August 29, 1896, a Chinese chef in New York invented chop suey. We "occident-ally" came across this delicious tidbit of information. When you serve chop suey, get the kids to help you think up the kind of sayings you might find in a fortune cookie. Write them on slips of paper, put them in a bowl, and let everyone draw out one and read it at dinnertime. This might "occident-ally" lead to a fun evening!

AFTER THE FEAST IS OVER

If you get tired of taking care of the fresh herbs left over from August 15, you can dry them in the microwave. Just remove the herb leaves—no stems. Measure 1 1/2 cups of leaves, and spread them on a paper plate or a double thickness of microwave-safe paper towels. Zap on high power for 4 or 5 minutes, stopping to stir several times during the drying. If you have a smaller amount, it might take less time. You can then store them in an airtight container and use whenever you want to spice up a meal and remember Mary's feast.

A SECOND CHANCE ON THE TWENTY-SECOND

If you didn't manage to get the family rosary started on August 15, you can try again today because August 22 is another Mary feast, the feast of the Queenship of Mary.

LOOK OUT! THE ZUCCHINI ARE COMING

This is the time of year when anyone who has a garden suddenly has an overabundance of zucchini. And they are likely to come bringing a bagful to your door. Once you've fried it, baked it, and thrown the rest of it out, they bring you *more.* So if your family likes apple butter, here's an easy surprise recipe to make mock apple butter using zucchini!

mock apple butter

Peel, seed, and coarsely chop zucchini until you have 4 cups. Put the zucchini into a blender with 4 tablespoons of vinegar. Blend until smooth. Pour the mixture into a saucepan, and add 1 teaspoon of lemon juice, 2 cups of sugar, 1 teaspoon of cinnamon, and 2 drops of red food coloring. Simmer for a long time, about 3 to 3 1/2 hours, until it gets thick. Cool and refrigerate. Serve with bread and butter and see if anyone can guess how you made it.

This is a good reminder of how you sometimes get a gift from God that you don't like at first, but if you use a little imagination and let it simmer long enough, you can turn it into something surprisingly delicious.

THE PATIENCE OF A SAINT

And you thought *you* had problems? She had a hot-tempered husband, a cantankerous mother-in-law, and a wayward son who was a real "problem" child. But her patience, perseverance, and prayer paid off. Who is she? Saint Monica. And her feast is celebrated on August 27.

Whenever you get discouraged remember Saint Monica who prayed for her family for years. Her pagan husband finally was converted before he died, and her son redirected his love of life to live a life of love. And he is now known as Saint Augustine. His feast day is August 28.

This is a special mother/son day so take a son to lunch—just the two of you. Tell him he is not a problem child, but you will always pray for him anyway. Make this a yearly occasion. If you have more than one son you might have to make it an ice-cream treat instead of lunch, but find time to take each of them for a one-on-one outing on a day near these saints' days. Be sure to explain why you are celebrating—to honor Saint Monica and Saint Augustine. (And don't forget to plan a special mother/daughter one-on-one on her saint's name day too.)

FAMILY ALBUM

Kids love to look through the family album and see pictures of who looked how, way back when. On a day when there is nothing to do, suggest they make a *Catholic Family Album*. Help them cut out two squares of colored construction paper for the covers and several squares of white paper the same size as the cover for the inside pages. Tell them to draw a picture on each page: first, a picture of Jesus, then the apostles, then Mary and Joseph, the pope, your pastor or any priest, a nun, a favorite saint, or any others they think belong in their Catholic family. On the last pages, draw a picture of *me*, *my family*, and *other Christians we know*. When all the drawings are finished, assemble them inside the covers, punch two holes on one side, and thread ribbon or yarn into the holes to hold the album together. Glue a sticker on the front or draw a cross or decorate it in a way that they like. You might be surprised at who they include in their *family*. After they finish their *Catholic Family Album*, look through your own family album again.

Dinner by Candle Light. Have a candlelit dinner and surprise the kids with a candle salad. Put a leaf of lettuce on a plate, top it with a canned pineapple slice for the candle holder. Cut a banana in half, and stand the banana upright inside the pineapple for the candle. Use a toothpick to attach a maraschino cherry to the top of the banana for the flame. (See illustration.)

Soap Opera.
Question: Why did the robber take a bath?

Answer: Because he wanted to make a clean getaway.

On a hot summer night, let the kids get into bathing suits and take some soap and shampoo and use the garden hose to take a bath on the driveway and towel off in the garage. Maybe this will encourage them to make a complaint-less and happy getaway to bed.

_____

_____

_____

_____

_____

_____

_____

_____

_____

_____

_____

_____

_____

CLEAR SAILING

Since this is the time of year for sailboating, have a sailboat lunch. Open a can of soup but jazz it up by adding a sailboat. Cut a piece of toasted bread into a circle or canoe shape—whatever size will fit into your soup bowl. Cut a slice of cheese into a triangular shape, and "attach" it to a straw with a bit of peanut butter, then stick this "sail" into the "bread boat" and launch it on the soupy sea.

You could also make sailboat sandwiches. Mix up some tuna, chicken, or egg salad. Separate a hot dog bun into halves to make the boats. Scoop out some of the bread, leaving a shell. Fill the shell with the sandwich filling. Then cut a slice of cheese into the shape of a sail, and attach it to the boat with a pretzel stick.

While you're sailing through lunch, tell the children about the day Jesus and his apostles were in a boat. Recall how, after Jesus fell asleep, a big storm came along and the apostles got so scared they woke Jesus up and begged him to save them. Then ask the children to tell about times when they were scared, and remind them that we can always ask Jesus to help us.

SEPTEMBER

SEPTEMBER

Saints' Days

The end of summer already? Where did it go? Time now for Labor Day, back-to-school, back to learning and serious stuff. But also time to celebrate those last warm, honeyed days before winter with a dip in a pool, a book to read under a still-leafy tree, and some family field trips. And then there's that big, exciting day near the end of the month: the feast of Saint Wenceslas.

The 6 best words to use more often:

I admit I made a mistake.

The 5 best words to use more often:

You did a good job.

The 4 best words to use more often:

What do YOU think?

The 3 best words to use more often:

Let's work together.

The 2 best words to use more often:

Thank you.

The 1 best word to use more often:

We.

The best 1 word to use LESS often:

I.

GREAT BEGINNINGS

This is sure to be a *great* month since it starts with the feast of Saint Gregory the Great on September 3. This pope was known to be wise and just, giving generously to charities, ransoming slaves, feeding victims of a famine, and restoring ecclesiastical discipline. He set an example for other clerics to lead a holy life and chose for himself the title, "Servant of the Servants of God." This title has been used by popes ever since.

This is also the Gregory who began the kind of singing known as Gregorian chant. Have you ever heard this kind of music? There have been several popular "chant" recordings made recently by monks. Try to find one at the library or at a music store, and play it tonight during dinner.

BLUE MONDAY BECOMES A RED-LETTER DAY

On September 5, 1882, ten thousand working people turned out to march in America's first Labor Day parade in New York City. Ever since then, the first Monday in September has been set aside to honor those who labor for a living. Since this is usually a holiday, don't waste a minute of it. Get up early and start the day by going to Mass with the whole family. Stop at a fast-food place so no one will have to "labor" cooking breakfast. (And say a "blessing" prayer for those who do have to work this day.) You'll probably get together with friends or family for the traditional cookout or picnic later in the day, but make this a family tradition to start the day with Mass and breakfast. Ask the children to say a prayer of thanksgiving for whatever work your family does to pay the bills each month and for all the workers who "serve" your family: barbers, dentists, grocery clerks, mail carriers, school bus drivers, teachers—and fast-food cook-ers and servers!

BACK TO SCHOOL, BACK TO WORK

When the kids start back to school, start a habit of blessing them as they leave each day. Simply make the Sign of the Cross on each forehead with your thumb, and give each a hug. As they dash away, say a quick silent prayer asking God to watch over them this day. And maybe *you* might like to become a student too! Sign up for some course to sharpen whatever special talent God has given you. Or take a refresher religion course or join a Bible study group.

Christian Proverb: "An ounce of practice is worth a pound of preaching."

Batter Up and Out. Did you know that it was in September, 1845, when the Knickerbockers Baseball Club was founded? And why should you care? Because that was the first baseball team to play by rules. Some of their rules were a bit different from today. Underhand pitching was acceptable. A batter was out if a ball was caught on the first bounce. And the first team to score twenty-one runs won! Does that sound like some of the Little League games you've bravely endured? When it's time to attend another of those "fun" games, treat yourself by taking along a box of carmel popcorn and when you're not munching, pray for patience.

What you are is God's gift to you. What you make of yourself is your gift to God.

"Hate the sin and love the sinner." Gandhi

Tell your child (or your spouse) to pick a number from one to ten. Then give that many hugs and kisses.

On the night of September 13, 1814 a young lawyer named Francis Scott Key boarded a British battleship. This was during the War of 1812, and he was there to make arrangements for the release of a prisoner. But while he was on board, the ship began an attack on America's Fort Henry, and he was forced to stay on board the enemy ship all night while the battle raged. That night he wrote the song that has become the national anthem of the United States, "The Star-Spangled Banner." If the kids don't know the words to this special song, teach them so you can all sing out loud when you go to the ballgame.

FAMOUS QUOTE:
If you think education is expensive, try ignorance.

TEACHING MEMORIES

Since this is the time of year when the children come home with stories of the new school year, start a dinner discussion of "favorite" teachers. The kids will love to hear stories of the parents' favorite teachers, and this will jog them to tell about their own favorite teacher. Join hands and say a prayer for all teachers; those who have touched your lives in the present and in the past.

HAPPY BIRTHDAY, MARY

September 8 is the day set aside by the Church to celebrate the birthday of our Blessed Mother. Make it an annual tradition to invite someone named Mary to your house for a birthday celebration. Serve birthday cake, of course, and maybe the children would like to make birthday favors for all or a little gift for all the Marys. Instead of the usual blessing before meals, say a Hail Mary, and end the meal by singing a Marian song.

BYE BYE BUTTERFLIES

Most of the butterflies will soon be gone from your yard so maybe the kids might like to make some butterflies for the Mary birthday celebration. They can cut some from construction paper and decorate. Or another easy way is to use those plastic fasteners that are on the top of a six-pack of canned drinks and some brightly colored pipe cleaners. Each plastic fastener will make three butterflies. Just cut the plastic horizontally into three sets of double circles. Trim around the edges a bit, then twist the top of each pipe cleaner to make "antennae," and staple it in the middle of the wings. You can also staple on a length of yarn, tied at the top, and you will have a hanging butterfly…or a butterfly on the wing. (See illustration.)

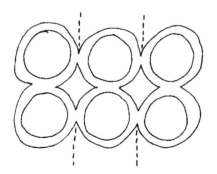 

THE SECOND SUNDAY

Set aside the second Sunday of September to celebrate Grandparent's Day. If the grandparents live nearby, invite them over or invite them out for dinner. If they live far away, send them cards or letters. They always love personal notes or drawings from the children. Or call to wish them a happy day. To instill in the children the value of family life, try to include grandparents, uncles, aunts, and cousins in as many family activities as possible all during the year. If there are no relatives nearby, "adopt" an older couple and include them in your gatherings. Always remind the children that even if they belong to a very small personal family, they also belong to the very large family of God and the Church.

PAN FOR GOLD ON SEPTEMBER 13

This is the feast day of Saint John Chrysostom, a bishop who was given an unusual nickname. This saint was such a wonderful speaker that he was called Chrysostom which means "golden mouthed." Are there any golden mouths in your family? If you know of one, do you think he or she might get a new nickname? Talk to the children today about the Golden Rule, and explain that we should always treat others the way we would want them to treat us.

A VERY GOOD SIGN OF FAITH

September 14 is the feast of the Holy Cross. If you don't have a cross or crucifix in your home, this is a good time to buy one and hang it in a place of honor. There are some beautiful small crosses made for children's rooms, and you could shop for those and hang one over your child's bed. This is also a good day to remind the children, again, to always make the Sign of the Cross reverently.

September 15 is the feast of Our Lady of Sorrows. Time for more teaching. Teach the children the five Sorrowful Mysteries of the rosary, and talk about what they mean. To refresh your memory, they are: the Agony in the Garden, the Scourging at the Pillar, the Crowning with Thorns, the Carrying of the Cross, the Crucifixion and Death of Jesus.

Forgiveness is the perfume that a trampled flower gives to the foot that crushed it.

Holy Halo. Don't forget September 29, the feast of the archangels: Michael, Gabriel, and Raphael. Michael the archangel, is often pictured wearing a shield and carrying a sword like the knights of olde. In fact, he was the patron saint of knights and warriors. In this day of so many warriors and super heroes on television, be an angel and tell the kids about this holy defender. And serve up some angel food cake. It has few calories so you can add lots of ice cream and chocolate syrup.

Bedtime. When you read a favorite bedtime story to your child, substitute the child's name for the main character's name in the book. Or make up your own stories in which your child is the hero or heroine. This will make bedtime stories more special and more fun.

Seeing Stars. When your child does something noteworthy (gets a good grade on a paper, scores in a ballgame, wins a spelling bee), the next day cut out a sandwich in the shape of a star to put in his or her lunchbox. Add a note that says, "You are our star!" If your child buys lunch at school, serve star cookies and milk at bedtime with the same message.

From Start to Finish. We act on our beliefs. Our actions form habits. Our habits form character. Our character leads to our final destination. Which way is yours leading?

A famous epithet reads, "Here lies an atheist. All dressed up and nowhere to go."

BUENOS DIAS

September 16 is celebrated as Mexican Independence Day so this would be a "mucho" good time to have a *so-long-summer Mexican fiesta* with Mexican food and recorded mariachi music. In Mexico, they are so proud of their Catholic faith that they have many religious processions right down the main street of town, often in the evening, with bands playing and people praying. And as the procession moves along, they set off firecrackers. How proud are we of our religion? Proud enough to march down the main street of town, praying and singing?

TAX RETURNS?

September 21 is the feast of the most famous tax collector, Saint Matthew, who changed careers and became an apostle and evangelist. So "tax" your brain, your energy, and your talents today, and think of some goals you or your family could have for the year to come. Should someone change careers? Should someone learn how to fill out tax forms? Should you use "tacks" to put up a memo reminding someone to start sitting less and moving more? Or maybe you should become an "evangelist" and try to talk someone into moving less and sitting still and praying more!

TWINS AND NO EXTRA CHARGE!

September 26 is the feast of two saints who were twin brothers, Cosmas and Damian. They were both skilled doctors and were venerated in the East as two of the "moneyless ones" because they treated the poor but did not charge them a fee! Ask the children to say a prayer today for all doctors that they will not only be skilled but also Christlike when they treat patients.

HOORAY FOR SAINT VINCENT DE PAUL!

Even his friends thought he was grouchy and irascible but with prayer and the help of God's grace, he changed and became a tender-hearted, affectionate man who was very sensitive to the needs of others. And then he became a saint! Honor him on his feast day, September 27, by giving a donation of some canned goods or a used but usable household item or a small check to the Saint Vincent de Paul Society. They carry on this saint's work by helping the poor.

"Christianity is like one beggar telling another beggar where he found bread."

D. T. Niles

HERE IT IS!

Are you ready? It's September 28 and the feast of Saint Wenceslas. "Good King Wenceslas" was murdered by anti-Christian forces one day on his way to Mass and now, for some reason, we sing about him at Christmastime. Although this is a bit early to be thinking about Christmas it seems an appropriate time to consider whether you spend too much money on materialistic gifts for such a holy season.

Before anyone starts shopping this year, have a discussion with family and friends, and suggest that the adults give each other only token or gag gifts and use the money they would usually spend on expensive gifts to pay off a family debt or to give a surprise gift to someone. They might give a microwave oven to an elderly couple who are having difficulty cooking three meals a day. Or buy new toys and take them to a children's home. Or ask a nursing home for the name of someone who never receives a gift, and send them a big bouquet of flowers to be delivered on Christmas Eve. At Christmastime when you open the gag gifts, anyone who wants to, can reveal how they chose to spend the saved money. Exchanging these stories will probably be much more memorable than the traditional gift exchange. Then when you sing the Wenceslas song it will have a whole new meaning.

Just Because. Leave a small surprise gift for your child (or your spouse) in a surprise place: in a pocket, on the bathroom mirror, under a bed pillow, in a shoe. When he or she asks, "For me? Why?" the answer is, of course, "Just because I love you."

Safety First. Have you ever had a fire drill at your home? If not, maybe you should. Talk about fires and explain carefully to each child which exit is best, depending on which room you are in if a fire starts. Tell them to get out first and then run to a neighbor to call 911. Then, one day when no one is expecting it yell, "Fire drill! Now!" and see how everyone reacts. If they don't react as you taught, go over it again. It's better to be safe than to wish you had thought of this.

Finding Time. Question: How do you find time to have so many family celebrations?

Answer: I let something less important go undone.

Besides, there are 1,440 minutes in each and every day. You just have to decide which is the best way to use them.

TEACH THOUGHTFULNESS?

The best way to teach is by example. So when a friend is sick or "shut-in" with a broken bone or housebound by being a caregiver for someone else, let the children see that you care.

Ask them to help you select cards and other cheery "hellos" to send in the mail: a photo, a cartoon clipped from a magazine, a joke, a balloon with instructions to blow it up and then pop it to "blow away" the stress or distress.

Make a card and on the front, draw the numbers one through ten. On the inside, write "You can count on me" or "You can count on us." Include coupons good for some "service" your family is willing to provide. You could volunteer to mow the lawn, bring in the paper each morning, or take out the trash on trash pickup day. Call ahead and ask on which night company would be welcome at the house, and then rent a funny video and take it over with a snack. Or take over a casserole for supper plus a spare for the freezer. Or, for a caregiver, give them a "night off" by offering to care for their patient for a few hours.

If there are children in the "ailing" family, give them rides to school or to after-school activities or take them with you to a movie or for an afternoon in the park to get them out of the house for a while.

If you, through your own actions, teach your kids to be aware of others' needs and if you let them "help you help" other people, hopefully this will develop into a lifelong habit of thoughtfulness and Christlike charity.

OCTOBER

OCTOBER

Saints' Days

The frost is on the pumpkin so it's time to get out some costumes, collect falling leaves, celebrate Columbus Day, and watch out for those ghosts and goblins like: "if only," and "I shoulda," and "poor me."

WISE WORDS AND WORDS TO THE WISE

A PRAYER FOR SERENITY

GOD GRANT ME THE SERENITY
TO ACCEPT THE THINGS
I CANNOT CHANGE,
THE COURAGE TO
CHANGE THE THINGS I CAN,
AND THE WISDOM
TO KNOW THE DIFFERENCE.

TIME TO WING IT

October 2 is the feast of the guardian angels. This would be a good time to take the kids to the angelport and watch the *angels* landing. But since you can't do that why not take them to the airport and watch some *planes* landing. Talk about how you think angels wings must look different from airplane wings. Ask each child, "What do you think your own guardian angel looks like?" You might be surprised at a child's view of an angel. If the kids don't know or have forgotten the angel prayer, you'll find it in this book on March 25.

IT'S A ZOO IN HERE!

October 4 is the feast of Saint Francis of Assisi who, as most children know, was a friend to the animals. If you're very brave you could take the children to a pet store today to look at the cute and cuddly animals. But, if you already have enough trouble without little voices begging, "Please, please, can we take it home with us," it would be easier to visit the zoo. The animals there are not available to take home. A zoo trip could become an annual outing on or near the feast of Saint Francis. In October, the zoo may be a bit cool but also a lot less crowded than in the summertime, and that makes it more special and personal. For a snack, take along a small box of animal crackers for each child and one for the grownups too.

<u>Why Me, Lord?</u> With the leaves falling and the sky gray and a very busy fall schedule, have you had a few "poor me" days? How about taking a jar or box and labeling it "Poor Me." Every time you have one of those dreary days, put a dollar in the jar. When you have a tidy sum, you can reward yourself with a treat or you could brighten someone else's day by using the money to buy a gift or give a donation to a worthy cause. Either way, the "Poor Me" box will give you something to look forward to.

<u>The Posture of Forgiving.</u> Confucius said: "To be wronged is nothing unless you continue to remember it." Let go of all those "wrongs" you've been carrying around and your daily load will be much lighter. Without all that weight, you can hold your shoulders up straight, march forth with hope, and look much younger and thinner.

<u>Bundt-kin Surprise.</u> For a pumpkin dessert, simply make a Bundt cake according to package directions. Tint white canned frosting with a mix of red and yellow food coloring until it is bright orange. Frost the cake, then stick a piece of green construction paper in the middle for a stem and you have a Bundt-kin dessert.

On October 7, remember to say the rosary. It's the feast of Our Lady of the Rosary.

<u>Noble Name Dropping.</u> Some kids like nicknames and some don't. So try making up a *virtuous* name that fits each kid and see if they go over: Bill the Brave, Grace the Gleeful, Tom the Truthful, Harry the Honest, Sara the Sincere.

DO THE ELEPHANT WALK

As a follow-up to the zoo trip, show the kids how to make an elephant head. Start with a big brown grocery bag. Cut out eye holes and a nose hole. Cut up another bag into long strips, and roll several strips together to make a long, sturdy tube for the elephant's trunk. Tape the tube firmly together. Cut four slits on one end of the tube so they can be folded back like a flower petal. Insert the trunk into the nose hole and tape the petals firmly on the inside of the bag. Next, cut out some big floppy ears from another bag, and tape them to the sides of the bag. Now tell the kids to put on the elephant head and take an elephant walk around outside. This should amaze and amuse the whole neighborhood.

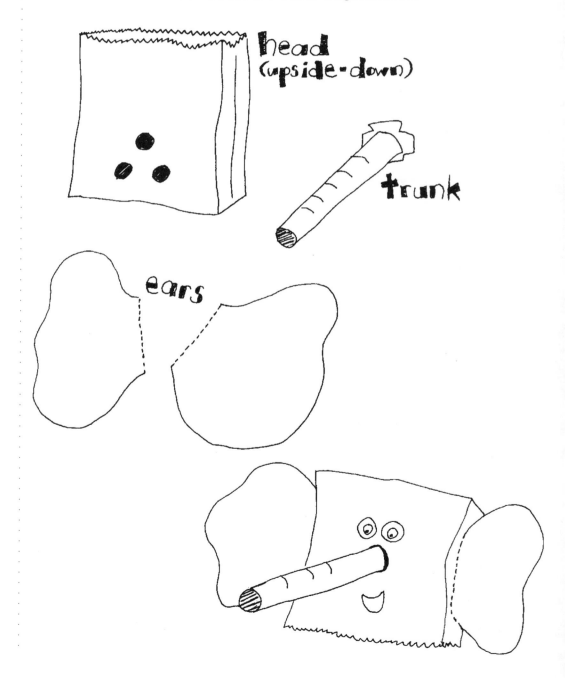

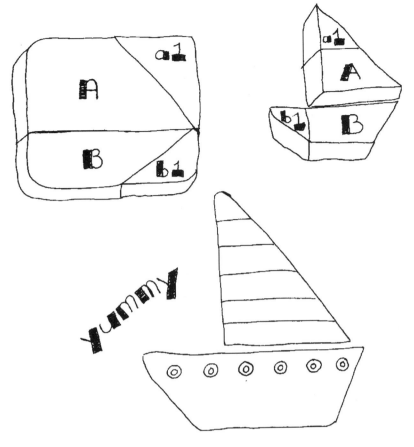

<u>Never Give Up.</u> October 28 is the feast of Saint Jude who is known as the patron saint of hopeless cases. If that diet just isn't working or those leaves aren't raked yet, say a prayer to Saint Jude today.

<u>Scary Suckers.</u> Show the kids how to make a ghost for your guests. Start with a round, paper-wrapped, "head-shaped" lollipop. Cover it with a white paper napkin or tissue. Tie around the "neck" with black or orange yarn. Draw on a ghostly face with a black magic marker. (See illustration.)

LAND HO!

In fourteen hundred and ninety-two, Columbus sailed the ocean blue. Today we honor him on October 12. What a great time to set sail on an adventure. If there's an aquarium in town, or a river or a lake, "voyage" there for some "watery" discoveries. If not, window shop at a boat dealer's showroom, and talk about how different today's boats are from those in the days of Christopher Columbus. Or just get out an atlas or any book you have about foreign lands, and talk about where you would like to adventure if you could sail to any strange, exotic spot in the world. Say a prayer for a safe journey for all who are on the road traveling somewhere today. If you feel like adventuring in the kitchen, let the kids help you make a Columbus cake. Just stir up a yellow or lemon cake mix. Pour half of it into a 9- by 9-inch square pan. Use the other half to make cupcakes. Bake according to package directions and cool. Cut and assemble as shown in the diagram above. Open a can of white frosting. Take out half and tint it blue with food coloring. Frost the boat blue. Frost the sail white. Or you can frost the sail in horizontal stripes of blue and white, but that's harder to do. Use the leftover frosting on the cupcakes. For portholes on the boat, use white, "life saver"-like candies.

Be Really Ghoulish. During October, give the kids a ghoulish giggle by asking them to help you dream up a dinner of "body" parts: ears of corn, finger sandwiches, hearts of palm, elbow macaroni, arm roast or eye of round, leg of lamb, tomaTOES! This will be a dinner they will remember and tell their friends about. They may even want to invite friends to share it. If your family has a strong stomach, you could also buy some plastic spiders and "swim" them in cups of cold apple SIDEr. Or you could put a candy GUMmy worm on each plate.

The bridges you cross before you come to them are usually over rivers that aren't there.

SPEAKING OF TRAVELING

Kids love secrets and mysteries. So turn your family into a secret society. Once a month, or whenever possible, suddenly announce that it's time for a mystery trip to a secret destination. No matter how much they beg, don't tell anyone where you are going until you get there. Just announce the time of departure. Sometimes it can be somewhere special, sometimes somewhere silly. If you can latch on to some cheap tickets, it could be a trip to the circus or a professional ballgame or a new movie. Another time, it could just be a trip to an ice-cream store for a cone or to a variety store or a hardware store where the kids get a dollar each to spend and thirty minutes to shop on their own. Or it could be a trip to Grandma's house or to visit a favorite friend. The destination will depend on the likes and dislikes of your own family. If you have a family with lots of dissimilar likes, you might want to only take one child at a time on an individualized mystery trip. Just be sure that each child—and each spouse—gets a turn. Always on the way home from mystery outings, tell the children to join in an out-loud Our Father in thanksgiving for having such mysterious and wonderful parents.

MORE SECRET STUFF

Since kids love secrets, learn how to say "I love you" in sign language, and teach them the signs. Then you can secretly send this message to each other any time, any place. (See illustration.)

I   L O V E   Y O U

OR

IS THERE A DOCTOR IN THE HOUSE?

October 15 is the feast day of Saint Teresa of Ávila, the kind of woman people do *not* forget. She was intelligent, charming, hardworking, and hardheaded but also very prayerful and holy. She founded convents and monasteries and traveled all over Spain accomplishing things at a time when most women never left their fireside. The letters and books she wrote still have appropriate messages for people today. All through history, many great Catholic religious leaders have been given the title "Doctor of the Church," but Teresa was the first woman to be given this prestigious honor. Have the members of the family make a list of who they think could be considered an important woman, both in the past and in the present. Many good mothers would properly fit on that list.

TIME FOR ANOTHER DOCTOR

Saint Luke was not a Doctor of the Church, but he was a medical doctor and a very important part of the early Church. His feast day is October 18. This might be a good week to take the kids to a hospital. No, not to the emergency room, but to the maternity floor. If you live in the same town where your children were born, take them to the very hospital where they were born, and if permitted, let them look through the glass at the new babies. Spend the rest of the time talking about the day each of them was born and how happy you were that God had sent you such a special baby.

<u>Pumpkin Pizza Too!</u> Buy a plain cheese pizza, a package of sliced pepperoni, and a green pepper. Before you bake the pizza, get the kids to help add a jack-o'-lantern face with the pepperoni slices. Cut some pepperoni pieces into triangles for the eyes and nose. Zigzag some for the mouth. Use strips of green pepper for eyebrows and hair. Use leftover pepperoni to make a circle around the outside edge of the pizza. Bake as directed. (See illustration.)

A Hair-raising Idea. To add excitement to a Halloween costume, here's a way to make your hair stand on end! Empty several packages of *unflavored* gelatin into a small saucepan. Add a little cold water, and stir over medium heat until the gelatin is completely disolved. Let the mixture cool to just warm, and use it to coat portions of hair, shaping it to stand straight up, swirl into huge loops. The hair will keep its shape when the gelatin dries.

"Marriage is the alliance of two people, one of whom never remembers birthdays and the other who never forgets them." Ogden Nash

Petite Pumpkin Dessert. At this time of year you often see tiny pumpkins for sale for decorating. Buy one (about 3 inches in diameter) for each family member. Pierce the bottom of each pumpkin with a knife in three or four places. Microwave on high for 6 or 7 minutes or just until tender when pierced with a fork or gently squeezed. Cool. Slice off the top and scoop out the seeds to make a shell. Put a scoop of ice cream in each and top with caramel syrup.

WE'VE CREATED A MONSTER!

Halloween has always been great fun for the kids but it's getting more and more popular with adults too. To keep in the spirit of things, you must decorate your house, dream up great costumes, have a party, and enjoy! And yes, you *can* do that. First, to save cut fingers, instead of *carving* a pumpkin, draw the outline of the kind of pumpkin face the kids like. Use a pencil to do this. It's a lot easier to make changes than with a knife. Once you decide on the design for the jack-o'-lantern, draw it on with permanent magic markers. An uncut pumpkin also stays fresh longer. For indoor jack-o'-lanterns, add strips of colored tissue paper for hair, paper circles for eyes, and a large pushpin for a nose. Look through your "bits and pieces," and make up some costumes or, if the kids insist, buy some inexpensive ones. But the homemade kind are more fun. If the kids go out trick-or-treating, you won't need to have a party for them; that will be fun enough. But you could have a party on the Saturday before Halloween for your silly adult friends. Invite them for a trick-or-treat dinner. If they want to come in costumes, that's great. If not, that's okay too. Plan a simple menu: store-bought lasagna, green salad, green peas, rolls, dessert, and coffee. Get a friend to help you "serve," and both dress as waitresses. When the guests arrive, serve snacks and drinks. While they are snacking, pass out "menus" for dinner and let them order six items. The "trick" is that the menu will be in code. (See example on page 95.) If they order Coffin Splinters, Ocean Spray, Jolly Green Ghouls, Skeleton's Coverup, Devil's Staff, and Pregnant Pumpkin's Desire, their dinner will consist of toothpicks, salt, green peas, a napkin, a fork, and a pickle! Someone else might get lasagna and a salad but no fork. After everyone has a good laugh at what they ordered, bring out the rest of the food, and let them help themselves. This sounds silly but it's easy to do and lots of fun.

Trick or Treat Menu

1. Devil's Staff
2. Pregnant Pumpkin's Desire
3. Coffin Splinters
4. Ocean Spray
5. Jolly Green Ghouls
6. Hot Stuff
7. Skeleton's Coverup
8. Dracula's Roman Holiday
9. Pumpkin Patch Cold
10. Vampire's Black Passion
11. Tootsie's Tumble
12. Grave Digger Mini
13. Goblin's Seesaw
14. Up a Creek
15. Mother Nature's Fool

Good Luck!

Fill in six selections.
You will be served exactly what you choose—no more, no less.

1. _____

2. _____

3. _____

4. _____

5. _____

6. _____

Name: _____

(Now just sit back, relax, and put on your funny face! Happy Halloween!)

Trick or Treat Menu—Control List

1. Devil's Staff: fork
2. Pregnant Pumpkin's Desire: pickles
3. Coffin Splinters: toothpicks
4. Ocean Spray: salt
5. Jolly Green Ghouls: peas
6. Hot Stuff: pepper
7. Skeleton's Coverup: napkin
8. Dracula's Roman Holiday: lasagna
9. Pumpkin Patch Cold: salad
10. Vampire's Black Passion: black olives
11. Tootsie's Tumble: roll
12. Grave Digger Mini: spoon
13. Goblin's Seesaw: knife
14. Up a Creek: water
15. Mother Nature's Fool: margarine

NOW BACK TO THE KIDS

If you do not want the kids to go out for the traditional trick-or-treating, you could get together with three or four other families and have a progressive party. At the first house, the kids arrive all excited and you take pictures or use the video recorder to film them in costume. Have a few snacks and a warm punch (cranberry and apple juice warmed with some cloves and a cinnamon stick). As you leave, the kids get treats for their goodie bags. At the next house, you get mugs of hot soup (made from canned or packaged soup) and salad. As you leave, the kids get goodies from this host and hostess too. At the next house, you have ready-made deli sandwiches or pizza, and maybe bob for apples or play a game. Again, the kids get treats at the end. At the last house you have dessert and coffee, more treats for the kids, and then head for home.

So what about the religious feast? It's hard to talk about religion in the midst of all the Halloween festivity, so earlier in the month, have a pumpkin dinner, and use this family time to talk about Halloween being All Hallows Eve—the night before All Saints' Day. You might talk about each person's name saint and even suggest that the children dress up as a saint. Some Catholic schools have an All Saints' Mass where the children come dressed as their favorite saint. It's fun to see all the "bathrobed" and "sandaled" saints, all the little "Marys" dressed in blue with white veils carrying a baby doll "Jesus," and all the bishops with cardboard bishop hats.

NOW ABOUT THAT PUMPKIN DINNER

Since you won't have to carve out a jack-o'-lantern for the pumpkin dinner, scoop out a small or medium-sized pumpkin for dinner to use as a serving dish. Cut off the top of the pumpkin and thoroughly clean out all the seeds. Then use it as a soup tureen. Just fix your family's favorite soup and pour it in. Add the top, sit it on the middle of the table, and supper's ready. Or fill the empty pumpkin with ready-made or homemade beef stew. Or mix up your favorite glop: browned ground beef, macaroni or rice, tomato sauce, onions, garlic, green pepper, or whatever your family likes mixed together. Spoon it into the pumpkin shell and replace the top. Put the pumpkin on a foil-lined baking sheet or pan, and be sure to add a bit of water in the bottom of the pan. Bake in a preheated 350° oven for about one hour or until the pumpkin insides get soft. Don't bake too long or the pumpkin will fall apart. Use hot pads to remove the pumpkin to a serving plate and won't everyone be surprised!

NOVEMBER

NoVembER

Saints' Days

1 **All Saints' Day**
2 **All Souls' Day**
3 **Martin de Porres**
4 **Charles Borromeo**
10 **Leo the Great**
11 **Martin of Tours**
12 **Josaphat Kuncevych**
13 **Frances Xavier Cabrini**
15 **Albert the Great**
16 **Margaret of Scotland**
16 **Gertrude the Great**
17 **Elizabeth of Hungary**
18 **Rose Philippine Duchesne**
21 **Presentation of Blessed Virgin Mary**
22 **Cecilia**
23 **Clement I**
23 **Columbanus**
24 **Andrew Dung-Lac and Companions**
30 **Andrew**

The saints are marching in, the Pilgrims are landing, and it's time for a royal feast: not only on the fourth Thursday—Thanksgiving—but also on the last Sunday of the month—the feast of Christ the King. November is a ripe harvest of days for family gatherings and giving thanks.

If you spot a November scarecrow, ponder what Thomas Huxley said: "Logical consequences are the scarecrows of fools and the beacons of wise men."

I hear and I forget. I see and I remember. I do and I understand. Just "telling" children is never as effective as showing them—and then helping them learn to do it for themselves. Working alone is sometimes much easier, but working together teaches—and can be more fun too. Be thankful this month that we are all lifelong teachers AND learners.

WHEN THE SAINTS GO MARCHING IN

The day after Halloween is a dull day because everybody is suffering from sugar overload. But it is a holy day so be sure to gather the family to go to church. On the way there or back, start a discussion about what a saint is and what "saints" you have known: a revered relative, a devoted neighbor, a special friend. It will be interesting to see who the children think of as modern saints.

REQUIESCANT IN PACE (MAY THEY REST IN PEACE)

On November 2 we celebrate All Souls' Day. So when you say the blessing before dinner, add a prayer for the repose of the souls of the faithful departed. As a centerpiece, you might put a few framed photos of family members and friends who have died, interspersed with some lighted candles or vigil lights.

THANKSGIVING IS COMING

Since this is the month when we think about giving thanks, you might start a house rule about saying thanks when someone gives you a present. Very polite and perfectly normal children today seem to have great difficulty writing a thank you note or even making a thank you phone call for gifts received. A good rule to make is this: When you receive a gift, you can't wear it, use it, spend it, or play with it until you have written a thank you note. Post the rule on the refrigerator and talk about the importance of gratitude and thoughtfulness. And once the rule is made, enforce it.

> When you receive a gift, you can't wear it, use it, spend it, or play with it until you have written a "thank you" note.

Say What? It's impossible to *really* listen and talk at the same time!

The secret of a good marriage is continuing to believe that the other will do better tomorrow.

"Art, like morality, lies in drawing the line somewhere." G. K. Chesterton

Room for One More. Some families make it a tradition to always invite one or more extra guests to share in their Thanksgiving, someone who is alone or lonely, a foreign student studying in this country, a military trainee, someone who has no relatives nearby, or someone who would just be fun to have around.

Adopt-a-Couple. Some families make it a tradition to choose one elderly couple or one newly married couple alone in a new city and include them in all of their holiday celebrations, making them "adopted" members of the family.

<u>Cran-sandwiches.</u> If you have leftover cranberry sauce, try spreading it on a cream cheese sandwich or on a turkey sandwich.

<u>A Scents of Thanksgiving.</u> If you live near some pine trees, take the children on a pine hunt. Let them snip small bits from the branches and enclose a bouquet in a small sealable plastic bag. Make enough bags to give one to each Thanksgiving guest as a take-home favor. Suggest that whenever they want to think of Thanksgiving Day, they should open the bag, sniff the pine, and imagine that they are in New England watching the Indians come over a hill to join the Pilgrims for that first feast of gratitude.

<u>The Turkey Trot.</u> If you're not too busy you could get the kids to help you make the orange cups described in February and fill them with cranberry sauce—one for each guest.

Some weeks you really need a Sunday on a Wednesday.

THIS IS YOUR LIFE

The feast of Saint Martin de Porres is celebrated on November 3 and his life story is a special one. His father was a Spanish knight and his mother was a freed black woman from Panama. When Martin was only twelve years old, his father arranged for him to be apprenticed to a barber-surgeon, and he learned the simplest form of the healing arts: how to set bones, dispense medicines, bandage wounds. But through this work, he also learned that he wished to devote his life to serving others. He became a Dominican religious brother and worked in the infirmary, helping the sick of the city and also the African slaves who were brought there. He soon became known for marvels of healing and works of wonder. As word of his good deeds spread, his father, who had become the governor of Panama, tried to get him to abandon this religious life. But Martin continued helping the poor and the sick as long as he lived. With some less-than-admirable sports and entertainment figures being "worshiped" as role models today, it is a gift for us that the Church has so many brave and selfless saints for children to learn about and imitate. Encourage the children to read about the lives of the saints often and to think of them as the best kind of role models.

TRY, TRY AGAIN

"The Christian ideal has not been tried and found wanting. It has been found difficult and left untried." G. K. Chesterton

PANTRY PARTY

When there's a rainy day and nothing to do, head for the pantry. Pick out three or four items that come in parts or pieces: a box of macaroni, a loaf of bread, a jar of pickles or olives, a bag of cookies. Challenge the kids to guess how many items are in each container. You can set a timer to tick off however many minutes you want them to spend on this. And then, of course, you'll have to take apart everything to count and find out who won. Once the packages are opened, you might have to have a dinner of macaroni with pickle and olive sauce, slightly fingerprinted bread, and cookies for dessert. And what does the winner win? That's up to you. But while you're counting, you can remind the kids to "number" their blessings as well.

WHO GETS YOUR VOTE?

Since November is election time in our country, have an election dinner. Plan this ahead and tell the kids to think about what *office* they would like to run for. Stress the fact that this does not have to be a political office but it can be. They can run for president, pastor, traffic cop, dishwasher, clown, astronaut, mother, father, anything. Some may choose not to run. For those who do want to run, tell them to prepare a campaign speech telling how they would change things or what they would do to improve things if they held the office they have chosen. They might want to make campaign buttons or posters and pass them out or hang them in the house. Have an all-American dinner: hot dogs, hamburgers, or pizza with ice cream for dessert. After dinner, let the speeches begin. Do not ridicule, but you can laugh if there is an appropriate time. Applaud and praise each speaker. If there were opponents, have a vote and see who wins, but give a prize (some small trinket or maybe candy jawbreakers) to all. Close with a prayer asking God to bless all our elected officials and help them to serve our country wisely and well.

HE WAS GRRRREAT!

Since the world today is very interested in science, the children might be interested to hear that one of the first and one of the greatest scientists was also a saint. He was known as Albert the Great, and his feast is celebrated on November 15. Albert spent twenty years writing a book about science, but the book also included information about some of his other interests: math, logic, metaphysics, politics, and astronomy. Ask the children, if they could make one great scientific discovery, what would they want it to be?

For the Brown Baggers. If a kid or spouse is already getting tired of whatever you put into the lunch bags, it's time for a bit of variety. Make a pita sandwich and remind them of the family pocket night last July. Or try a checkerboard sandwich. Just make any kind of sandwich but use one slice of white bread and one slice of dark bread. Cut the sandwich into fourths, then flip over two fourths to make a checkerboard. Send along a thermos of soup. Include small bags of popcorn or chow mein noodles or sunflower seeds.

Hurry, Hurry! To save time when making lunches, make up a batch of sandwiches twice a month and freeze them so they'll be all ready to just pop into a lunchbox or bag in the morning. DON'T freeze anything with mayonnaise, boiled egg, or jelly.

If you really want to keep fresh sandwiches cold, pack them with a frozen can of juice that will thaw by lunchtime. Also a vacuum bottle will keep dinner leftovers the kids like (stew, franks and beans, soup) warm until lunch.

THE PILGRIMS ARE COMING!

We all know that November is time to think about the Pilgrims and Plymouth Rock so this is the hour to talk about the Mayflower. Here are some facts to discuss with the kids this month: The Mayflower set sail from England in September 1620 and finally landed at Plymouth Rock over two months later. A two-month sea voyage might be fun today, but it was very dangerous sailing back then with no radio to signal for help and no helicopters to come to the rescue. Because of the danger, two ships usually sailed together but the tiny Mayflower sailed alone—a small ship on a big ocean. Would you have been afraid? Would you have prayed?

It was very crowded. On this tiny ship, there were 102 people (including 32 children) plus the captain and a crew of about 26 men. No one had expected the ship to be so crowded. Some of the passengers had planned to sail on a different ship but it leaked, so they were added to the Mayflower passengers. Would you have hated to be so crowded?

It was very scary. Since the ship was made of wood, everyone was afraid of a fire on board. When the sea was calm, they cooked food in metal boxes filled with sand; but if there was wind, they ate cold food. Would you have been afraid of fire or more afraid of eating bad food?

It was very dirty and they had very bad weather. No one could take a bath or change clothes. Because of the stormy weather, the ship rocked and rolled and passengers got seasick. Would you have gotten sick and tired of this trip and wished you had stayed home?

After discussing the Mayflower, say a prayer of thanksgiving for our brave forefathers and foremothers, and pray that you will be as brave when you sail forth into the unknown future.

IT'S TURKEY TIME

In the United States, we take a day off on the fourth Thursday of November to give thanks for the harvest, for our family, for God's blessings. This celebration began way back with the Pilgrims, but it didn't become a national holiday until 1863. And it only happened then because of a lady named Sara Josepha Hale. She was one of the country's first lady editors, beginning with *Ladies Magazine* in Boston and then *Godey's Lady's Book* in Philadelphia. She wrote editorials for forty years urging that, as a nation, we set aside a certain day for all to give thanks. Finally, President Abraham Lincoln issued a Thanksgiving proclamation, and we've been giving thanks together in November ever since. Something that might be even more interesting to the children is the fact that Sara Hale also wrote "Mary Had a Little Lamb." If you are having guests for Thanksgiving the kids might get a kick out of singing this song and then telling the guests about Sara. They also might like to make up a special blessing to be said before the Thanksgiving feast. You could help them with this, but they might make up a great prayer all on their own.

ANOTHER FAVOR?

The kids do love to make favors, and here's a really easy one to give each guest for Thanksgiving. Have your child trace his or her hand on a square cut from a sturdy brown grocery bag. The thumb will be the turkey's head and the fingers the tail. Decorate the tail feathers with bright crayoned stripes, add an eye, feet, and a red wattle (this is the red thing that hangs from a turkey's neck). Draw a wing in the palm area. Instead of a grocery bag, the kids can draw on sturdy white paper and color the turkey brown. Or they can draw on small brown lunch bags and give one to each guest to use to take home foil-wrapped turkey leftovers from dinner. While the kids are working on this, remind them that we use our hands and our hearts to serve and love God. Also remind them to tell the guests that these are real *handmade* favors.

Winter Wonderland. For an easy winter centerpiece, buy some coarse sea salt (you can find it in the grocer's spice section with the table salt and pepper), and put it in a low, clear glass dish. Set white votive candles on top of the salt to make an inexpensive fire-and-ice centerpiece.

Cinderella Time. When a little girl in your family has a birthday or any special day to celebrate make a princess cake. Just bake a packaged Bundt cake according to the directions. Unmold and set on a serving plate. Put a 10- or 12-inch doll in the hole in the center of the cake. Frost the cake and add splashes of colored sugar to make it look like a ball gown.

Notes

_____

_____

_____

_____

_____

_____

_____

_____

_____

_____

_____

_____

_____

_____

_____

_____

_____

_____

THE BIRDS GET HUNGRY TOO

This is the time of year to feed the birds, so during the Thanksgiving holiday the kids could make their own bird feeders. Since it's also the time of year for pine cones, take a pine cone and firmly attach a string to the top with a loop long enough to hang it from a tree. Spread the pine cone with peanut butter, and then roll it in birdseed or sunflower seeds which will stick to the peanut butter. Hang the cones outside, and watch the birds flock to eat. Talk about how God must have made birds to decorate the sky.

LITTLE PITCHERS HAVE BIG EARS

When you're talking to a friend and know your child is nearby, brag a bit about something good that your child has done or some talent he or she has, loud enough so the child will "accidentally" overhear you. Kids like to hear good things about themselves but don't like to be embarrassed by your making a big thing of it when they are present.

A ROYAL FEAST

On the last Sunday in November we celebrate the feast of Christ the King so it's time for a royal dessert. Buy a cheese cake, or any cake, and two boxes of _pirouette_ cookies. Spread some canned icing around the side of the cake, and press the cookies so they will stick and stand up all around the cake. Then take a yard or two of wide pretty ribbon, and tie it around the cake and make a pretty bow.

DECEMBER

DECEMBER

Saints' Days

3   Francis Xavier
4   John Damascene
6   Nicholas of Myra
7   Ambrose of Milan
8   Immaculate Conception of the Virgin Mary
11 Damasus
12 Our Lady of Guadalupe
12 Jane Frances de Chantal
13 Lucy
14 John of the Cross
21 Peter Canisius
23 John of Kanti
26 Stephen
27 John, Apostle and Evangelist
28 Holy Innocents
29 Thomas Becket
31 Sylvester I

Last but certainly not least, December is that wonderful month of sleigh bells ringing, snowflakes glistening, "Silent Night," and a miracle birthday. That would certainly be enough reason for celebration but there's more. This month includes days to honor Mary, an apostle, and lots of saints. And one of those saints is (ho ho ho) Saint Nicholas.

Deck the halls with boughs
of laughter,
fa la la,

'Tis the season to be holy
and happy—not harried—
fa la la,

Join we now our friends and family

and

Join we now our hands in prayer.

BEING PART OF THE "RIGHT" CIRCLE

You probably already know all about the Advent wreath and have one in place in your home, but just in case you haven't started this tradition, here's how: Simply buy an Advent wreath at a religious goods store or a gift shop. Or make a wreath of greenery. In the greenery, place four candles: three purple and one pink. You can use votive lights to be safer if you have small children. If you can't find the colored candles, use four white candles, but tie on ribbon bows: three of purple and one of pink. Each night before dinner, say a short prayer or read a bit of the Christmas story from the Bible. The first week, light one purple candle; the second week, light two purple candles; the third week, light two purple candles and the pink candle; and by the fourth week, when you light all four candles, you know Christmas is near. Each week of Advent has a theme—first, expectation; second, joy; third, hope; fourth, acceptance. The circle of the wreath reminds us that God's love surrounds us and is never-ending. The greenery signifies new life. The purple reminds us that Advent is a time to ask for and give forgiveness. And the pink tells us Advent is a time of joy and hope as we await the coming of Jesus.

ADVENT PRAYER

Here is a simple Advent prayer for children: Dear Jesus, thank you for coming to earth to show us how to live. We are getting ready to celebrate your birthday on Christmas. We love you. Amen.

PUT OUT YOUR SHOES?

In some countries, children put their shoes outside the bedroom door when they go to bed on December 5. On the morning of December 6, the feast of Saint Nicholas, they find a few pieces of candy and a tiny toy in the shoes. In some areas, gifts are given only on Saint Nicholas Day and Christmas Day is kept sacred as a religious holiday. Isn't that a good idea?

Mr. D. Halls. Knock, knock. Who's there? Dexter. Dexter who? Dexter halls with boughs of holly. Fa la la la la, la la la la.

<u>Have a Ball!</u> It was an old custom, at this time of the year, to make spice balls by sticking whole cloves into apples or oranges and then hanging them around the house to give it a nice homey aroma for the holidays. To make a longer-lasting one, let the children stick cloves into a styrofoam ball. Use a small ball so the kids will not get tired of the project. When it is entirely covered, tie a pretty ribbon around the ball with a loop for hanging. (These would also make nice small Christmas gifts for the children to give to relatives, but if you make them ahead of time, seal them in an airtight plastic bag so they won't lose the scent before you give them away.) Note: you can find whole cloves in the spice section at the grocery store.

ChristExtmas Tree Candle Holder. Core an apple, making a hole large enough to hold a candle. Stick sprigs of evergreen into the apple until it is completely covered, then add the candle. You may have to put a bit of modeling clay on the bottom of the candle to make it stand straight. The juice from the apple will keep the evergreen fresh for several days.

Deer Favors or Gifts. Here's an easy way to make a reindeer. Twist a colorful pipe cleaner around the curve of a candy cane. Cut another into two pieces, and twist them around the first to make the antlers. Glue on wiggly eyes which you can buy at a craft store and a red pompon for the nose. Tie a ribbon around the deer's neck, and add a jingle bell.

A SWEET STORY

There is a sweet legend about Saint Ambrose, whose feast is celebrated on December 7. The story goes that when Ambrose was a baby, he had his mouth open, babbling happily as babies do, when a swarm of bees flew down and settled on his tongue. His mother was terrified of course. But the bees did not sting the baby or fly down his throat. Instead, they left a bit of honey on his tongue and flew away. The legend says that this was a sign that Saint Ambrose would grow up to be a bishop and a great preacher who spoke with a "honeyed" tongue. Tell the children this story today while you munch on peanut butter and honey sandwiches.

MOTHER'S DAY IN DECEMBER

December 8 is the feast of the Immaculate Conception. In some countries this is celebrated as Mother's Day, so it's a good day for all the family to go to an evening Mass and then go out to a fast-food place for dinner so Mother won't have to cook. On the way to or from church, how about saying a decade of the rosary together in the car.

THE WASSAIL BOWL

When the kids' friends come visiting during the holidays, serve your own idea of wassail: warm apple cider, or cranberry-apple juice warmed with broken pieces of cinnamon sticks. Tell them wassail means "Be in good health," and invite them to say a prayer for anyone who is sick.

JINGLE A NEW TUNE

Ask the kids to help you write your own funny, family lyrics to the tune of a popular Christmas carol: Jingle bells, jingle bells, here comes Tommy White. He wears jeans and likes green beans and howls at the moon at night. Sing these during the holidays, and save them to bring out every Christmas to sing again and giggle again and maybe rewrite.

COOKIE CATS

December 13 is the feast day of Saint Lucy. In some countries, Lucy is honored as a patroness of school girls, possibly because she was martyred when she was a young girl. And, since school girls like to play with kitty cats, it is the custom to serve Saint Lucy buns which are

shaped like cats with raisin eyes. Since you have nothing else to do in December(!), you could buy some large round cookies, use a tube of cake frosting to draw on the shape of a cat, and serve Saint Lucy cat cookies today.

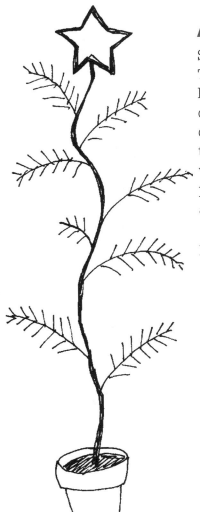

A CUSTOM-MADE TREE

Some families have a *memory* tree. They might have a fancy tree in the living room and put this sentimental one in the family room. They decorate it with whatever is special to them: a bit of lace from a wedding gown or veil, baby pictures, school pictures, badges or awards won by the children, an old collar from a well-loved dog or cat, a packet of rubber bands from the orthodontist after the braces have come off, a bracelet from a hospital stay, a piece of a cast from a broken bone, a spark plug or license plate from an old but loved car, a golf ball. Once you start this, you can save things all through the year and keep adding to it so that every year you can "remember when" every time you look at it. One newlywed couple didn't have any ornaments yet so they decorated a tree with favorite Christmas cards. This became their tradition.

<u>Deer Wrapups Too!</u> To "deerly" decorate a package or make a card, cut a large and a small triangle from a brown grocery bag. Cut four strips from black construction paper for deer legs, and glue on the package or card. Glue the large triangle over top of the strips for the body. Turn the small triangle upside down, and spread glue along the sides but *not* on the top. Place the point of the small triangle over the point of the big triangle, and glue this on for the head. For antlers, put glue on two twigs and tuck them under the top, unglued portion of the small triangle. Draw on black eyes and a red nose or glue on a red cinnamon candy for the nose. (See illustration.)

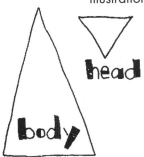

Deer Cake Too! Use a lamb mold to bake a cake. Frost the cake with light chocolate icing. Add a cherry nose and make antlers with broken pieces of curly pretzels. (See illustration.)

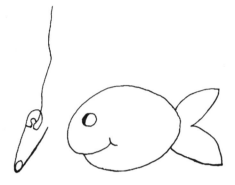

Go Fish! December 27 is the feast of Saint John the Apostle. Since some of the apostles were fishermen, tell the kids to "go fish" today. Cut out some fish from construction paper, and cut out a big eye hole on each. Mark the underside of each fish with a different number. Put the fish in a box, give the kids a string with a safety pin tied to it, and let them try to hook a fish by getting the safety pin into the eye hole. When they're all fished out, add the numbers on the caught fish and see who has the biggest catch. Serve tuna sandwiches and say a prayer thanking Saint John for being such a good apostle.

KEEP THOSE KIDS BUSY

Since kids love Christmas and love to help, what are some easy things they can do to be a part of your Christmas preparations? If they're old enough, ask them to help address Christmas cards or at least glue on the stamps or return address stickers.

They can help make angel cookies: Buy a roll of refrigerator cookie dough, and cut it into 1 1/4-inch slices. Cut one slice with a triangle center to make the body and wings. Cut another slice into fourths and use one fourth to roll into a ball for the head. Assemble as in the illustration. Bake and ice.

Roll up red cloth or paper napkins, and tie with green ribbon and a bit of holly or a jingle bell to use for a family dinner or a party.

Make a macaroni ornament: String red yarn through pieces of uncooked macaroni to form the shape of a wreath, then tie a bow on top. (See illustration.)

Make a ribbon wreath: Buy a small styrofoam or wire wreath or a small embroidery hoop. Cut equal lengths of colorful leftover ribbon, and tie them on.(It was an old custom to embroider initials or the first name of family and friends on thick good quality ribbons and make a friendship wreath of them, adding new names each year.)

Unwrap and assemble the Christmas crib figures. If you don't have a crib set, take the kids shopping to buy one. After you assemble it, gather around in a family prayer circle and sing a carol (possibly "Silent Night").

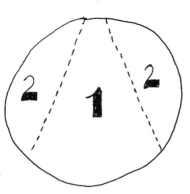

ANGELS WE HAVE HEARD ON HIGH

Since angels are very popular at Christmas, suggest that the kids add angel "wings" to a favorite doll or teddy bear by cutting wings out of white fluted paper plates. Or one of your "little angels" might make a Christmas angel's harp. Just stretch rubber bands around a lidless shoe box. Use fat bands and skinny ones so they will have a different sound. Try arranging them until you have a "scale" (the big bands make low notes, the skinny bands make higher notes). Pluck these strings with fingers or rub the back of an old toothbrush across them.

SPICE FOR THE SPOUSE

Start a tradition with your spouse. Suggest that each year you give each other a Christmas card and enclose something as a reminder of your year together: ticket stubs from some event you both enjoyed, a packet of sand from a happy day at the beach, a napkin from a restaurant where you had a date. Once you start, you can save something to give each year.

PARTY TIME

Make the table festive by putting greenery, like a wreath, around a serving plate. Add a few fresh cranberries to look like holly berries. Make a "wreath" of lettuce leaves or parsley on a tray and add munchies: red radishes, cocktail tomatoes, green olives, fresh or pickled mushrooms.

Sprinkle a dessert with white chocolate "snow." (Rub a room-temperature bar of white chocolate over a large-holed grater. Collect the "snow" on waxed paper, and chill until ready to use. For larger shavings, scrape the white chocolate bar with a vegetable peeler.) Put all sizes of lighted candles burning around the house, including some scented ones, for atmosphere.

FESTIVE LIGHTS

In addition to the traditional visit to see Santa, take the kids for a ride to look at the Christmas lights around town, and stop at several different churches to say a prayer by the Christmas cribs.

A Fun Gift That Will Say Thank You. As a stocking stuffer or an after-Christmas gift, give each child, depending on their age and likes, a box of personalized or pretty stationery. Add stickers, crayons, and fancy pens. Maybe this will make it fun for them to use their gift to write thank you notes for all their other gifts.

Our Family Footprints. On the last Sunday in December we celebrate the feast of the Holy Family. For a centerpiece for your Sunday meal, have the kids make each person in the family stand on a brown grocery bag and trace his or her footprint. Cut out the footprints, and put them down the center of the table or around in a circle. Talk about how each member of the family leaves a different kind of print but how each is important and necessary. For the blessing, say a prayer for each person: Thank God for Daddy who is so good at reading bedtime stories. Thank God for Mommy who thinks of such good surprises. Thank God for Johnny who makes great kites.

Since there are probably some peppermint candy sticks leftover from Christmas, make a drum cake for dessert to strike up the band and say "Hooray for the family." Just frost a cake with white icing and press candy sticks into the icing at an angle all around the cake. Put a maraschino cherry at the end of each peppermint stick. **[See illustration]**

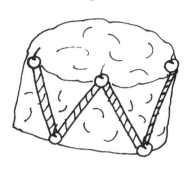

CHRISTMAS EVE

Since you will be feasting tomorrow, plan a simple meal for Christmas Eve, and make it a tradition to always serve the same thing every year. In Mexico, families often make large quantities of tamales to serve during the holidays so maybe you might want to have canned chili and tamales as a contrast to the usual Christmas fixings. Or you might want to have cold meat and cheese with a fancy bread. Did you know the word *Bethlehem* means "house of bread"? Find some kind of very special bread the family would like and always serve it on Christmas Eve or Christmas Day, reminding them of Bethlehem.

STAINED GLASS

For an easy family dessert that will be a bit religious, make three batches of gelatin—lime, orange, and strawberry—using 1 cup of boiling water but only 1/2 cup of cold water for each. When they are chilled, cut into cubes. Fill dessert dishes with some cubes of each color, and tell the kids this is to remind them of the stained glass windows at church.

AFTER CHRISTMAS

Take lots of family photos during the holidays. When you have that after-Christmas letdown, spend an evening with the family looking at all the photos and picking out your favorites. Put these into a Christmas scrapbook, and let anyone add a note or stickers or drawings about this Christmas. Save the scrapbook, and add to it every year.